# The Art and Skill of Successful Negotiation

# The Art and Skill of Successful Negotiation

## John Ilich

Prentice-Hall, Inc.          Englewood Cliffs, New Jersey

Prentice-Hall International, Inc., *London*
Prentice-Hall of Australia, Pty. Ltd., *Sydney*
Prentice-Hall of Canada, Ltd., *Toronto*
Prentice-Hall of India Private Ltd., *New Delhi*
Prentice-Hall of Japan, Inc., *Tokyo*

Fifth Printing . . . . . May, 1978

**Library of Congress Cataloging in Publication Data**

Ilich, John
    The art and skill of successful negotiation.

    1. Negotiation.    I.   Title.
BF637.N4I44            158              72-14166
ISBN 0-13-046805-3

Printed in the United States of America

*If it is not right, do not do it;*
*if it is not true, do not say it.*
Marcus Aurelius

# *How This Book Will Benefit You*

Negotiation is probably one of the most common forms of human contact in the world today. Its importance and direct relationship to success in life is, therefore, not confined solely to professional activities but must necessarily spill over into every conceivable form of human contact. People of all ages, in all places and, indeed, at all times gather together to "talk about it" in order to reach a common ground.

Very early in my professional life I sensed the importance of this established form of human endeavor and its direct relationship to success. It fostered within me the urgency to develop an expertise in the art and skill of negotiation. This urgency was also facilitated by the numerous and varied negotiation situations that I was exposed to daily.

The basic purpose and ultimate objective of any negotiation should be the attainment by the negotiating sides of a successful conclusion. Otherwise, there would be no genuine purpose for meeting in the first place. One should never presuppose, however, that the attainment of such a successful result can be left to fate, chance, or even some mysterious process of osmosis or other similarly unrealistic circumstance or happening. On the contrary, the most skillful and thus the most successful negotiators are those who have working for them very definite and refined principles, strategies and techniques.

In this text I have set forth carefully developed principles, strategies and techniques in the art and skill of negotiation that have carried me successfully through hundreds of negotiations, many of which were not only highly complex but the outcome of which also involved many millions of dollars. This is a text designed to be put to actual, practical application. The principles,

11

strategies and techniques are refined and explained in easy to understand language to facilitate ease in application and reference. In addition, the book is appropriately dispersed with actual, living experiences to fully bring to life and illustrate many of the principles, strategies and techniques, and to show how they can work for you in actual practice.

For purposes of clarity and in order to distinguish between the negotiating sides, the terms "negotiator" and "opponent" are frequently used. The reader should recognize, however, that in many negotiating circumstances the parties may not be truly adverse and, in some instances, even very friendly, but still striving to reach a common understanding on a matter important to both.

In many negotiations the negotiator may be representing a "client." The term is intended to apply to any situation where the negotiator is negotiating for someone other than himself. In addition, the reader should always bear in mind the distinction between a negotiating principle, strategy, and technique. A principle is a negotiating rule of conduct, such as the maintainence of outstanding character and integrity by the negotiator. A strategy is a plan of operation, and a technique, the method used to carry out the plan of operation. The use of repetition would be an illustration of a negotiating technique.

As earlier related, knowledge of successfully proven negotiation principles, strategies, and techniques is an essential part of every deliberation, discussion, or conference that involves people and requires them to get together to bargain, sell or engage in business transactions. Whether you are negotiating an important merger, a large tax matter with the Internal Revenue Service, buying or selling a home, or perhaps merely settling an overdue debt with the plumber, you can put these successfully tested and proven principles, strategies, and techniques to work for you. With proper application they can give you that competitive edge which so often means the difference between success or failure.

John Ilich

# Contents

How This Book Will Benefit You ..................... 7

1. The Meaning of Art and Skill in Negotiations .......... 17
2. Time and Place to Negotiate ....................... 21
3. Presence of the Negotiator's Client .................. 25
4. The Negotiating (Physical) Environment ............. 30
5. The Negotiator's Mental Attitude ................... 33
6. The Negotiator's Physical Appearance and
   Mannerisms .................................... 35
7. The Stick Theory of Preparation.................... 39
8. Priority of the Five Negotiating Senses ............... 45
9. How to Develop a Good Negotiating Memory.......... 49
10. Language of the Negotiator........................ 52
11. The Need for Objectivity.......................... 56
12. Pre-Negotiation Organization ..................... 58
13. Selection and Use of Assistants.................... 62
14. Knowledge of Procedure.......................... 65
15. The Importance of Maintaining Negotiating
    Bases......................................... 68
16. Habit (Friend or Foe) ............................ 73
17. The Use of Correspondence in Negotiation ........... 77
18. Commencement of the Negotiation.................. 82
19. Offensive Negotiation ........................... 85
20. Why It's Important to Determine Who Has
    Final Negotiating Authority ................... 89
21. Your Opponent.................................. 94

22. Appealing to the Self ........................  98
23. The Place of Anger in Negotiation................. 102
24. The Necessity for Equalization .................... 107
25. Avoiding the Danger of Inversion ................. 111
26. How Anxiety Can Affect a Negotiation............. 113
27. Simplicity ....................................... 118
28. Timing ......................................... 120
29. The Importance of Observation.................... 123
30. When to Take "No" for an Answer................. 126
31. Principle vs. Personality........................... 128
32. The Influence of Repetition in Negotiation .......... 133
33. Adding New Elements ........................... 136
34. The Art of Extrapolation......................... 139
35. The Question Method ........................... 141
36. The Art of Flowing Through...................... 147
37. Emotional Appeal............................... 149
38. Silence ......................................... 155
39. The Warmth of a Smile ......................... 156
40. Disposing of Potentially Troublesome
        Arguments ................................. 158
41. Building Goodwill............................... 161
42. Use of Demonstrative Exhibits .................... 164
43. Making the Offer or Counter-Offer ................ 167
44. Setting a Precedent ............................. 170
45. The Importance of Maintaining Control ............ 174
46. Avoiding Predictability .......................... 178
47. When to Intentionally Break Off Negotiations........ 183
48. Jest and Earnestness ............................ 186
49. Closing the Negotiation.......................... 189
50. Experience vs. Repetition ........................ 193
51. Broadening the Negotiator's Educational
        Base ...................................... 195
52. Prayer......................................... 198
    Index........................................... 199

# The Art and Skill of Successful Negotiation

# 1

# *The Meaning of Art and Skill in Negotiations*

*"For any systematic treatment of a subject should begin with a definition, so that everyone may understand what is the object of the inquiry."*
Cicero

Once, after I had successfully completed the negotiation of a large and important matter, my happy client, after expressing his gratitude, asked, "What's your secret?" Since we were both running short of that precious commodity called time, I advised him that it would take a while to explain and that perhaps at a future date I might put it all down in writing. I've endeavored to do that in this work; but first let's begin with that definition.

The words "art" and "skill" are easy to understand when associated with such matters as playing the piano, painting a masterpiece or even gourmet cooking. But do they mean the same in negotiation? Perhaps their most accurate and certainly their most applicable meaning to negotiation is the ability to do something well. In order to develop that ability there must be great practice, dedication and sacrifice. In the end, however, like Leonardo da Vinci, who was able to capture on canvas a precious masterpiece like the Mona Lisa, the negotiator may be able to attain his own masterpiece in the form of a successful agreement.

The word "negotiation" can best be defined as a "conferring between individuals." Whenever more than one person is involved, it means that the relationships can be as delicate as the stroke of that of a master painter like Leonardo.

To put the words together, we could confine our definition to the ability to confer between individuals. But is that all a master painter needs to know, how to apply the paint to the canvas? Isn't the mental process of creating the picture and selecting the paint equally important, or perhaps even of greater importance? It's here then that we must search for our real definition.

## How to Determine the Merits of a Position

Before an individual can be persuaded, the merits of any position must have been fully demonstrated to him or he must be otherwise motivated, perhaps through his emotions. When a negotiator is demonstrating, he is actually in the process of applying the paint to the canvas. He does this by his spoken words, physical gestures, use of exhibits such as photographs, and even by silence. But just like the master painter, before he can attempt to demonstrate, he must first determine by his inner creative process what the picture will look like and what tools will best do the job. In other words, before the negotiator can adopt a strategy or use a technique, he must first answer within himself: What will it be? Why should I use it? When should I use it? How should I use it?

The answers, of course, will largely govern the negotiation's outcome. If the negotiator is consistently successful in reaching the answers to these questions, he's truly mastered the art and skill of negotiation. If not, he can touch the canvas as often and with as many different colors and kinds of paints that he wants, but he'll never be able to come up with that masterpiece.

The real definition then of the art and skill of negotiation is: The *mental* ability to *observe* and *put into practice* the *best* means of persuasion in *any* given situation. It's important for anyone aspiring to master the art and skill to understand the full impact of this definition and to carefully read the entire text that follows in that light. He can thus weave the various principles, strategies and techniques into his own way of thinking so that when it comes time to apply them, he can answer the questions of what, why, when and how successfully.

Unfortunately, there is no short cut to learning, nor does one success make an individual proficient. On the contrary, the important thing is consistency. To attain it takes great patience. The negotiator must also be long on courage, an indispensible quality that must be developed. He must be a confident person, confident in his own abilities and his ability to persuade. He must be flexible. Most of the situations that he encounters will present him with alternate possibilities. His mind must be quick and alert, and he must possess mental toughness. Negotiation is no place for the gullible or the timid. He must be thoroughly prepared and he must be enthusiastic.

The principles, strategies and techniques that I've set forth in this book will provide the negotiator with the finest paint, brushes and canvas to work with. The creative process necessary to apply them, however, must come from within himself. Negotiation is generally a free-wheeling affair, with no formal rules to serve as guidelines and often with no holds barred. The twists and turns that may occur can often be greater than the path a climber must take to reach the top of the highest mountain peak. Each situation is different and often beyond the complete control of the negotiator. Predicting with certainty what will happen is therefore an impossibility. With nothing to direct him except his own personal character the negotiator must resort to the one weapon that, if properly trained and utilized, will serve him best—his mental ability. It goes without saying that with the proper training and application of his creative process, he will possess the ability to observe the best means of persuasion in any given situation and put into practice the most effective principles, strategies and techniques; for if he adopts an inferior means, he may fail, and if his opponent comes up with the superior means, he may emerge the victor. It's bad enough to fail, but even worse to lose!

## How to Hold Up under Pressures of Negotiations

People frequently ask me about the pressures associated with negotiation. They're there and very real. But the skillful negotiator should consider them as part of the challenge in mastering the art and skill.

One of the most indispensible requirements in mastering the art and skill of negotiation is to develop a keen understanding of human nature, and it's equally as important to know yourself. The old adage that, "He who knows and knows he knows is a wise man" is particularly applicable here. Know your strengths and weaknesses. Work to apply your strengths to their greatest advantage. Overcome your weaknesses until they become strengths. If you don't, some shrewd opponent will soon discover them and use them to your detriment. Learn to recognize your opponent's strengths, and to equalize them and to capitalize on his weaknesses.

One of the most important goals that the negotiator must set for himself is to build a bridge of trust between himself and his opponent. There's no established formula to attain it. It simply means that he must conduct himself in such a manner that everything he does or says is above reproach. By building a bridge of trust he will be providing himself with immense latitude in the discussions. Virtually everything that he says or does will go unquestioned. This doesn't necessarily mean that his opponent will agree with it, but it does mean that he'll accept it as being fact. Contrast that with a situation where everything the negotiator says or does must be substantiated.

Finally, many struggle to succeed in negotiation but never really know why they fail. Others may not fail but never know why they succeed. Learn to master the art and skill as I have defined it so that you can do both, succeed and know why.

# 2

# Time and Place
# to Negotiate

Is there an ideal time to negotiate? How about an ideal place?
I've been asked those questions often. My usual response is "Yes."

## When to Negotiate

The first important point to remember is that whenever
practicable, the negotiator should select both the day and time of
day that are most suitable to his personal make-up. Each individual has a certain body metabolism together with traits and habits
that largely govern his actions. If he's a late riser, for example, and
doesn't get rolling until, say, after lunch, he should try to do all of
his negotiating later in the day. If he frequently takes catnaps and
wakes up fresh and invigorated, he should do his negotiating then.
Perhaps he never works on Sundays. Seldom is it wise in such cases
to set up an important negotiation early Monday morning when he
may not have had sufficient time to get back into the swing of
things.

When travel is necessary, try to allow time to rest after arrival
rather than rushing right into the discussion. One of the easiest
ways to fluster a negotiator is to get him into serious discussion
when you know he is not ready. If that happens to you, back off
and tell your opponent that you will need five or ten minutes or
even several hours, if necessary, to collect your thoughts.

Learn to judge how much breakfast, lunch or dinner to eat
prior to any discussion. Food will temporarily dull the senses.

21

Hence, never overeat or consume too much heavy foods such as pastry or potatoes. Eat lightly, and if you must eat plenty, concentrate on lighter foods such as seafood or lean meats. If you're negotiating during lunch or at any other meal, which is often the case, be certain to eat sparingly. Let your opponent fuel up. It'll slow him down and perhaps tip the scales in your favor.

Similarly, you're not ready to negotiate if you have a splitting headache or other ailment that will not allow you to fully concentrate. Recognize that the nature of the ailment is relative to the importance of the negotiation. A severe headache or cold, for example, would probably be sufficient to call off an important negotiation but not settling an overdue debt or reaching a price on the cost of constructing a home.

A second important point to remember is that although ideally it is best to select the time to negotiate, often this is not practical. The negotiator should, therefore, be fully prepared to negotiate at any time and never lose what *he considers to be* an opportunity to negotiate. Let me explain more clearly what I mean by relating a personal experience. Negotiations had been previously carried on to arrive at the fair market value of the stock of a closely held corporation. The final price, however, had not yet been determined. I happened to have a chance meeting with my opponent on the street. He was going one way and I the other, both on wholly unrelated business. We chatted for no more than a minute and agreed on the price. The matter was well along and all of the facts and law were fresh in my mind. The time was, therefore, right to negotiate. If I would not have been prepared, I would have greeted him warmly but tactfully suggested a later time to discuss it.

I have negotiated at almost every imaginable time and day—early in the morning, afternoon, late evening, weekdays and weedends—but I've always observed the above premise.

From what I've said, I think it's apparent that the ideal time to negotiate is *any* time that the negotiator is able to be at his maximum effectiveness. The best rule to be guided by is: *Never lose an opportunity to negotiate, but never negotiate until you are certain it's an opportunity.*

## Where to Negotiate

Whenever possible, the negotiator should select the place to negotiate. One reason why trial lawyers are sometimes not good negotiators is because they are accustomed to working in the courtroom, where the drama is controlled by rules and procedures which are enforced by the presiding judge. Negotiation, on the other hand, is generally free wheeling with no holds barred. The more control the negotiator can exercise over the negotiation, therefore, the better, and this includes selecting the place. The next time your opponent asks you, "Where shall we meet?" be prepared to tell him.

The best place to negotiate is on the negotiator's home field. If he has an office, in his office. If he travels by airplane and frequently stays in hotels and motels, then in the hotel or motel. If he travels by car, then perhaps sitting casually in the front seat of the car. If he sells homes, then in the home he is attempting to sell; if the negotiator is a housewife, in her home. The reason is similar to the advantage enjoyed by a football, baseball or other sporting team playing on its home field. It's a familiar environment where most of his preparation has taken place. He can thus concentrate more on the game rather than burning up energy adapting himself to the new surroundings. To a negotiator whose mind may be crammed with facts, law, strategies, and techniques, the home field can offer a tremendous advantage. His memory will generally serve him better since many associations have been formed during his preparation. In addition, his train of thought and coolness under fire are apt to respond better because of his prior experience on the home field.

Recognizing, however, that it may often not be possible to pick the home field because, as I have already related, the time to negotiate is whenever the negotiator is at his maximum effectiveness, the negotiator should always try to be fully prepared to negotiate virtually any place. I have negotiated in airplanes, hotels, motels, restaurants, and even subways and taxicabs. Here again, the rule to be guided by is: *Never lose an opportunity to negotiate, but never negotiate until you are certain it's an opportunity.*

A skillful negotiator will often attempt to catch his opponent off guard by pinning him down in a strange place when he least expects to negotiate. Maybe it's happened to you? Don't let it happen again. The next time either be fully prepared to negotiate or gracefully suggest another place—preferably your home field. If that's not possible, pick a neutral site. The last choice should be your opponent's ballpark.

# 3

# *Presence of the Negotiator's Client*

The decision as to whether a negotiator's client should be present during the negotiation is an integral part of any negotiation strategy and must be considered in the early stages of preparation. No firm rule exists. Nevertheless, definite consequences can and do flow from either his presence or absence, and several important considerations should be understood.

### Why Clients Should Not Be Present

One of the most important reasons for excluding the client from the negotiation is because he is generally inexperienced in negotiating strategies and techniques, and often unaware of the legal consequences of what he might say. The opponent may thus level his attention directly toward the client and gain valuable admissions or concessions which ordinarily could not have been obtained. One recent experience will illustrate how this may occur.

My client had entered into a long term lease on a large piece of improved real estate. Circumstances later developed whereby it became paramount that the rental be reduced. The lease contained both a minimum rental plus a gross rental based upon sales over a certain dollar volume. After careful examination of the lease, it became clear that there would be no way to reduce the rental on purely legal grounds. The landlord was not in default and, in fact, had honored the lease to the letter. An alternate strategy had to therefore be used. After consideration, it was decided to call in the landlord's attorney and to suggest a conference on the matter. He was also requested to ask his client to attend.

During the first half hour of the session there was little progress, the landlord's attorney making it clear in no uncertain terms that there existed no legal basis for the reduction, and none would be given. The client interspersed his attorney's position with comments of his own and finally concluded with the fact that he was an "honorable" businessman and always tried to do what was right. The opening was immediately sensed, and the next ten minutes or so were spent discussing *directly with the landlord* the need for honor in business and that not only was his honor not being questioned, but that both he and my client were honorable and would be dealing together for many years either directly or indirectly, since the lease was of long term; and, finally, that we were asking him as an honorable man to exercise his fairness by granting the reduction. Needless to say, both the landlord and my client were well pleased—the landlord, with the opportunity to demonstrate his honor; my client, with the very much-sought-after rent reduction.

A second important consideration for not having the client present is that his absence will shield or insulate him from the discussions and thus afford him the opportunity to enjoy good relationships with the other side. This takes on added emphasis when the negotiations are heated or adverse, as may often be the case. The client, in effect, makes his negotiator the "fall guy" and is generally free to carry on friendly relationships long after the matter has been concluded, regardless of whether a successful agreement has been reached.

Still another consideration is that the negotiator has full leverage to conduct the bargaining as he sees fit, using whatever strategies and techniques he desires within the guidelines dictated by his client's objectives. This provides the negotiator with much more flexibility. To illustrate: if the negotiation has reached a stalemate, with both sides standing firm on their respective positions, the negotiator may ask his opponent to fully state his position, together with the reasons, with the comment, "I'll present it to my client, but I doubt seriously whether he'll go along because . . . " The negotiator then proceeds to state the reasons why. This can not only be a very effective method of keeping the negotiation alive, but is also a way to keep the client shielded.

When relating the objections or reservations to his opponent's position, the negotiator may proceed to add objections or reservations which may be of no important consequence to his client. By this method he accomplishes several essential objectives. First, he has apprised his opponent that when they meet again there exists a very real possibility that his opponent will have to give on some or all points. Second, when the negotiator returns to the bargaining table with the expected announcement that his client cannot go along, he may begin by conceding one or more of the objections raised at the previous conference which were of no real significance to his client, thereby making it appear as if he has altered his position favorably to his opponent. Following this up with a reasonable counter-offer can and often does lead to surprising and very favorable results.

Finally, actual presence of the client may have an effect on the negotiator's concentration, particularly if the negotiation is complex and lengthy and requires a great deal of preparation and mental retention. Irrespective of what may have been written about men such as Napoleon, who was reputed to have been able to dictate five letters simultaneously, the human mind can *effectively* concentrate on only one subject matter at a time. The only real exception to this phenomenon, if one can call it that, occurs when an action or thought becomes very habitual, thereby freeing the mind from concentration. If the negotiator is thus consciously aware of his client's presence, he may be hampered and his attention diverted by fear that his client may inadvertently say or do something detrimental to his own cause. Moreover, the negotiator may be reluctant to go all out in order to avoid embarrassing his client by his firm handling of the bargaining, language, or attitude, or may proceed very cautiously in order not to present himself in an unfavorable light to his client.

## When the Negotiator's Client Should Be Present

There exist several situations where the presence of the client is necessary. The first and most obvious is when the client desires to conduct the discussion and has requested the negotiator to be present in order to advise him on legal matters or other sticky problems which may arise. Care should be taken here to distinguish this situation from that of the normal procedure of having the negotiator conduct the discussion. In this latter situation the negotiator should undertake complete charge of the negotiation, including the decision as to whether the client should be present. In the former the client assumes full responsibility and, in effect, becomes the negotiator. This situation is fairly common, particularly among non-complex business matters. I do not recommend it, however, when the matter to be negotiated involves highly complex and technical matters or with definite legal ramifications, matters of great importance, or when an opponent is skilled in the art of negotiation.

Finally, another consideration where the presence of the client may be desirable and operate to effectively attain the desired result arises in what I like to refer to as the "two tier" conference. I call it that because it always necessitates at least two conferences to gain the desired objective. It most often occurs after the client has initially conducted the negotiations on his own and has been unsuccessful.

To illustrate, assume a corporation entered into a large business transaction which required a substantial cash commitment from the other side. Assume further that the commitment was never reduced to writing as it normally should be. When it comes time for the other side to honor their commitment they balk, and all efforts by the corporation to dislodge them meet with failure. In situations such as this a complete turnaround of the other side's disposition must ordinarily be accomplished in order to have any chance of success. Here's how it might be done.

The negotiator may request an initial conference, at which time he should take the opportunity to fully state the corporation's position and to firmly but reservedly point out that the next step may be appropriate legal action in the event the cash commitment is not met. (When using harsh words, never combine them with a harsh tone. The two are usually not compatible in negotiation. You're there to demonstrate, not to anger.) Since the negotiator was never a party to any of the previous discussions, his presence constitutes a new element. His remarks, therefore, should be limited to reiterating the corporation's position and the consequences in the event the cash commitment is not met. The corporation should not have a representative present at this initial conference.

Thereafter, a second conference should be set up at which a representative of the corporation should be present to again make his company's position known. The negotiator's presence at this second conference should serve to refresh the other side's recollection of the corporation's sincerity to pursue the matter to the end and thus strongly and favorably influence it in the corporation's favor.

Although I've used a corporate illustration in the above example, the same technique can be used in most situations where a debt is due and a party has previously conducted unsuccessful negotiations on his own.

# 4

# *The Negotiating (Physical) Environment*

Many of us visualize, when we think of negotiation, a scene where a group of men are gathered more or less formally around a large, polished table. Perhaps some are in shirt sleeves with ties pulled loose at the collar. Another may be driving home a point with his clenched fist pounding the table top like a stern judge's gavel as he demands order in the court. Fortunately, this is seldom the case. If a meeting of the minds had to frequently depend on such formality, man's daily activity could easily slow to a snail's pace.

Since the negotiator should take what he considers to be every opportunity to negotiate, regardless of the time or place, it is important for him to maintain flexibility with the negotiation environment. Nevertheless, here are some important considerations which should be observed whenever possible.

Always try to select a place where you will not likely be interrupted. Nothing is more exasperating than to be interrupted in the middle of a thought or phrase. This includes the telephone. It's impolite to take calls with your opponent sitting there while you're talking. Instruct your switchboard girl or secretary not to disturb you. If you are expecting important calls, always be considerate enough to advise your opponent beforehand. And after you've taken the call, be certain to thank him for his patience. He'll appreciate your thoughtfulness.

Try to select a quiet place. Noise may not only make it difficult to hear but will also interfere with your concentration.

If you're negotiating in your office or any other place where you have control over the physical environment, be certain that everything is very neat. Books should be in order and not sprawled all over the room. Papers should be stacked neatly. Similarly, papers in your briefcase should be well organized. Neatness will be a good reflection upon you and your habits. This includes your hotel or motel room or automobile, if that's where you're negotiating. Everything should be in order and you should know precisely where everything is. Nothing is more reflective than responses such as "I wonder where I put that?" or "Now where is that? I know it's around here somewhere." These are tipoffs to the skilled negotiator that his opponent may not be well prepared. Leave nothing to chance, particularly in important negotiations.

Know precisely where you will sit and where your opponent will sit. Pick a chair that's comfortable, roomy enough to permit shifting of the body in order to relax it. This will prevent fatigue, particularly in lengthy sessions. Be certain the chair has a fairly straight back and a firm cushion to prevent slouching and to allow full breathing. Proper breathing will help keep the brain functioning better.

Never sit in a chair that is lower than your opponent's! It should be at least equal and preferably higher. Nothing can dampen optimism more than having to look up throughout the entire negotiation. Sometimes a skillful opponent will deliberately set an individual in a lower position and glare down at him intently, sort of like the third degree in an old James Cagney or Humphrey Bogart movie. It gives him a psychological edge. Learn to recognize these situations and try to pick your position. If you find yourself in a lower position, do what I do under such circumstances. Spend most of your time standing and strolling back and forth in front of your opponent. He'll get the message and invite you to sit on an equal basis. And if he doesn't, you'll still be able to look down at him.

Finally, in selecting the setting always recognize that sometimes even the best laid plans can go astray. To illustrate, during the negotiation of a very complicated matter most of the discussion took place in a very large room, in the center of which was a large, oval-shaped table. I sat in the center. To my surprise, each of my opponents (there were two) seated himself at an end. There I was, sandwiched in the middle, unable to see one when I was looking and talking to the other. To make matters worse, it soon became apparent that they had prearranged a system whereby the one outside of my view could signal the other as the negotiation progressed. In addition, I discovered that both were close enough to see any papers that I set before me on the table and the one not within my view often attempted to exercise the liberty. Rather than change positions, however, I decided to embark upon a bold plan. During a break, I carefully culled my file and arranged in separate piles every piece of data that supported my position. These I freely laid on the table in front of me during the discussion. As I made a point to one opponent, the data was there before me for the other to see and to substantiate what I was saying, and thus strengthen my position. It worked so well I decided to remain there throughout the entire negotiation.

# 5

# *The Negotiator's Mental Attitude*

The human brain is a wonderful organ. It can make sense out of the most complex situations or it can wallow in a sea of uncertainty, unable to make even the most basic situations come alive, even though all the necessary tools may be there waiting to be put to their proper use. What, then, is the difference between these two situations? Why can one person of equal capability and experience outperform another? Often the answer can be traced to mental attitude.

*Before a negotiator can ever be successful in any negotiation, he must first believe that he can be.* E. H. Harriman, one of the nation's leading railroad pioneers and a man bubbling with self-confidence, once remarked to a young financier, "Let me be but one of fifteen men around a table and I will have my way."

Sometimes I have deliberately postponed a negotiation because I was not convinced in my own mind that my position was completely sound. What did I do? I went back to the drawing board, so to speak, and reviewed the entire matter. Perhaps I checked out new court cases which might shed some light or re-examined factual matter. I kept digging until I was fully convinced of the merits of my position. Otherwise, how could I ever hope to successfully demonstrate it to another?

### How to Develop a Proper Mental Attitude

One of the best ways to develop the necessary positive mental attitude is for the negotiator to practice it in virtually everything he does. Maintain such an attitude on small matters as well as large ones. A belief that one can make a simple tire change on a car, win at a friendly game of tennis or maybe even bake a delicious loaf of bread or tantalizing, mouth watering French pastry will foster the type of healthy mental attitude that will carry over into larger matters, such as difficult and complex negotiations. In short, it's virtually impossible to fully separate the negotiator's ordinary daily activities from his negotiation activities, simply because all involve either a greater or lesser degree of mental effort. One cannot, therefore, expect to maintain a positive mental attitude in negotiation and go around feeling pessimistic about everything else that happens in life. The converse, of course, is also true. And since one negotiates a relatively minor portion of his lifespan, it therefore follows that a good marketplace to develop that mental attitude necessary to successful negotiation is on the little, everyday tasks that one is confronted with.

A sound, positive mental attitude, standing alone, is like a flag without the pole. It's important, therefore, that a negotiator's belief be based upon substance and not fantasy. Hence, another excellent way to develop the necessary positive mental attitude is through thorough preparation. Knowledge that one is well prepared breeds confidence. The man who believes that he can climb a mountain can put his belief into actual practice by getting himself into superb physical condition, by undertaking such matters as making smaller climbs under circumstances that are similar to those that he expects to encounter, and by anticipating and learning how to deal with unfavorable weather elements that may greet him along the way. The same applies to negotiation.

In conclusion, a section on the power of positive thinking would not be complete without an appropriate story. One of my favorites occurred during the Second World War. When General Montgomery assumed the responsibility to drive General Rommel, the crack German general, out of Africa, he confided to a friend that a military leader's life was filled with great sacrifice and a career could be easily wiped out with one serious defeat on the battlefield. His friend attempted to console him by pointing out that he may very well defeat Rommel. "I wasn't talking about me," Montgomery replied. "I was talking about Rommel!" That's positive thinking—the kind that wins wars and negotiations!

# 6

# *The Negotiator's Physical Appearance and Mannerisms*

If you had a serious problem and walked into a lawyer's office to retain him, it would undoubtedly concern you greatly if he had on a rumpled, old, soiled shirt with frazzled collar and sleeves that looked as if he had slept in it. And if, immediately after you entered and began telling him your troubles, he sat in the middle of his desk with folded arms like an Indian chief in counsel, you might even panic. Both are obviously gross exaggerations. Nevertheless, they do illustrate the fact that how a person looks and acts has an important bearing upon his impact on others. It's no different in negotiation.

## The Negotiator's Physical Appearance

It goes without saying that the negotiator should look the part he's supposed to represent. The most essential point to always bear in mind is to project a natural image. This means that his appearance should focus attention on what he's saying and doing and not on what he's wearing. Clothes should usually be conservative, with no loud colors or color combinations. The key is naturalness. What's natural to one person, of course, may not be to another. A tall man wearing a suit two sizes too small will certainly have trouble projecting the proper image, whereas if the same suit were worn by the right individual the problem would disappear. Similarly, a short person wearing clothes that look as if they might have fit him before he went on a diet will encounter the same problem of focusing the opponent's attention on his appearance. In both cases there's no naturalness. Remember, how you look has an important bearing on how your opponent will react. If you look as though you know what you're talking about, that's the appearance you'll project and it'll greatly increase your effectiveness. If you don't, you will be making your job just that much more difficult.

While we're on the subject of clothes, one of the poorest practices is to remove the coat, roll up the shirt sleeves, and open the collar so that the necktie hangs loosely around the neck. I know of no quicker way to project a tired, listless image, even though you may be inwardly full of enthusiasm and eager to go (as you should be). Never neglect the fact that sight is an important means of communication, and during the course of much of the discussion the opponent's eyes will be fixed upon you. Hence, even if the negotiation is long and drawn out or the room or weather very warm, avoid this practice. If it gets too warm or you simply want to make yourself comfortable, remove your coat and tie and then loosen the collar. And if the sleeves must be rolled up, do it neatly and not during the discussion when it'll detract from what you're saying or take your attention from what your opponent is saying.

If you wear glasses, select the type of frames that fit the face and a color that's somewhat conservative, such as brown. Here again, you want your opponent to concentrate on what you're saying and doing, and not on what you're wearing.

In formal negotiations I would generally recommend a white shirt. It's neutral and thus goes well with most suits and ties. Also, in formal negotiations always greet an opponent with a coat and tie. If you later want to relax, follow the method that I've suggested above. This practice should be followed regardless of whether your opponent is "an old friend" or not. Never take him for granted.

Finally, a word about neckties. Wives (bless them) have a habit, for various reasons (most of which they never disclose), of picking up ties from time to time for such occasions as birthdays,

Father's Day, and anniversaries. I suspect there's always the hidden desire that they want their man to be the dashing, gay blade of a sort. The color combinations, sizes and shapes sometimes reach indescribable proportions. If you're fortunate enough to have a wife (as I have) who picks them as you want them, fine—no problem. If not, think of a million excuses why you can't wear any on negotiation day. One's bound to work.

## The Negotiator's Physical Mannerisms

Here again, the most important point to always bear in mind is to act naturally. People are generally quick to sense artificialness, and if an opponent feels he's being "put on," it will be very difficult to make any real progress. What usually happens in such situations is that the opponent will look upon each proposal very suspiciously and take a great deal of time to make up his mind before committing himself. This is why it's important for the negotiator to practice any desired hand, arm or other body movements until they reach the natural state. And it goes without saying that he may want to eliminate any of the bad habits which I will discuss more fully in a later section.

Gestures in negotiation should fit the subject matter of discussion. For example, when talking of a small or trivial matter, large, sweeping arm motions, fist pounding or other exaggerated movements may not only leave an awkward or artificial impression, but also unnecessarily precondition an opponent to such an extent that when it comes time to use them on a larger, more important issue, they've lost their impact. Conversely, smaller gestures on larger matters appear equally out of place.

The size of the room or other area of negotiation, such as an automobile or even outdoors, also has a bearing on the size or extent of any gestures. Generally speaking, the larger the area the larger the gesture. A sweeping arm motion while outdoors will normally go over well even though the issue may not be that large, whereas in a small room or automobile such a movement may easily appear exaggerated even though the issue may be large.

Good eye contact is an absolute necessity! Whenever you're making a point, look directly at your opponent, particularly on large and important matters. Looking away from him at such a critical moment may easily leave him with the impression that you really don't believe what you're advocating.

Using an object to make or emphasize a point is sometimes a good practice. An opponent will generally fix his sights on it as you're speaking and thus associate it with what you're saying. He thus has something more tangible to remind him of the point in addition to your spoken words, and when he's deliberating on his decision, particularly if he wants time to consider the proposal, he'll be much more apt to remember what you've said. A pencil in the hand is an example. But don't overdo it or use the technique too often. And once the point has been made, set the object down, preferably out of sight, unless the point you want to make is a very important one; in such a case it would do well to leave the object in a place for him to see and thus serve as an association device to refresh his recollection. If on a smaller matter, however, the object may detract from your opponent's concentration on other, more important matters you're advocating, and you may thus be doing more harm than good.

In concluding, I want to again emphasize that all movements should flow smoothly and naturally. As the mind functions, so should the body, so that any gestures become virtually automatic. If you do a great deal of negotiating and have not yet developed the technique of using the body for emphasis, I would strongly recommend that you practice before someone who can constructively comment on your naturalness or, if necessary, before a mirror. Do so until you've mastered this important aspect of demonstration.

# 7

# *The Stick Theory of Preparation*

Dr. Watson, the inimitable colleague of Sherlock Holmes, literature's most famous sleuth, was questioning the great detective about his knowledge of various subjects and was amazed to learn how remarkably little he knew of many. Watson's surprise was reported to have reached a climax when he found that Holmes was completely ignorant of the composition of the Solar System. When questioned about it, Holmes replied that he couldn't care less and that he would do his best "to forget it" now that he knew it. The dialogue continued:

"To forget it!" Watson exclaimed, quizzically.

"You see," Holmes explained, "I consider that a man's brain originally is like a little empty attic, and you have to stock it with such furniture as you choose. A fool takes in all the lumber of every sort that he comes across, so that the knowledge which might be useful to him gets crowded out, or at best is jumbled up with a lot of other things, so that he has a difficulty in laying his hands upon it. Now the skilled workman is very careful indeed as to what he takes into his brain-attic. He will have nothing but the tools which may help him in doing his work, but of these he has a large assortment, and all in the most perfect order. It is a mistake to think that that little room has elastic walls and can distend to any extent. Depend upon it—there comes a time when for every addition of knowledge you forget something that you knew before. It is of the highest importance, therefore, not to have useless facts elbowing out the useful ones." [1]

In order for any negotiator to be consistently successful at the art of negotiation, it is absolutely essential that he prepare thoroughly just as any champion must do in order to win and maintain his crown. Thorough preparation often entails the consumption of a considerable amount of time and the necessity to pour over volumes of written data, particularly if the anticipated negotiation is complex and one of great importance. If the negotiator feels that he can put anything and everything into his "brain-attic," he'll soon find that "useless facts" will be "elbowing out the useful ones," and he's likely to be in for a very disheartening experience at the bargaining table.

What I like to refer to as the "Stick Theory" of preparation evolved over the course of preparation for hundreds of bargaining sessions, and resulted from this need to prepare in as little time as possible yet maintain maximum effectiveness at the bargaining table. It has proved to be an invaluable preparation tool and has been successfully tested under the most difficult and complex situations, some involving many millions of dollars and as many as sixty to eighty separate negotiable issues. It can similarly work for you.

## The Basic Stick Theory

The Stick Theory is designed to focus the negotiator's attention as early as possible on only matters that are relevant to the negotiation. Imagine that the brain is truly an "empty attic" with room for only a minimum number of "sticks." The exact number is not important. What is important is for the negotiator to always strive to keep the number at a minimum.

In every negotiable issue, regardless how complex, there are only a very few fundamental areas around which it will ultimately be decided. These areas may vary with each different type of issue. Nevertheless, they're always few in number; sometimes only three

---

[1] Sir Arthur Conan Doyle, "A Study in Scarlet," cited by William S. Baring-Gould, THE ANNOTATED SHERLOCK HOLMES (New York: Clarkson N. Potter, Inc., 1967), Vol. I, p. 154.

or four, seldom more than twelve to fifteen. The initial step is to pinpoint these fundamental areas. They are the "sticks" which will be allowed into the negotiator's "brain-attic." His entire preparation is then centered around them. All data is quickly reviewed and only that which is relevant to each stick is retained. By this process of elimination he can quickly concentrate his study on only matters of relevance rather than ". . . of every sort . . . so that knowledge which might be useful to him . . ." doesn't get " . . . crowded out, or at best jumbled up with a lot of other things . . . ."

## The Stick Theory in Action

Let's take a common, everyday occurrence and see how the Stick Theory might apply. Almost everyone has the occasion to purchase a new or used car. Naturally we'd all like to negotiate the best deal possible, as would the car dealer. Here's how the task might be approached.

The fundamental areas in most car purchases are:
1. Gross price (includes extras such as air conditioning, etc.)
2. Trade-in value (old car)
3. Financial terms (if financed)
4. Service after the sale

These are the sticks around which all preparation should be centered. Gross price, trade-in value, financing and service after the sale can generally be obtained from the car dealers. Financial terms can also be obtained from other reputable organizations, such as banks or loan companies. A very simple process, yet one designed to limit the scope of investigation to only relevant matters and to point out the differences in costs. Setting the various dealer comparisons side by side should tell you in an instant which is offering the best deal. And taking the best to a reputable dealer of your choice will, in most instances, result in his even beating or matching it in order to keep pace with competition.

In order to more fully illustrate the Stick Theory, let's now focus our attention on a situation more conducive to negotiation. Assume that the negotiator has been retained to negotiate the sale of an interest in a closely held corporation. These situations are common and may arise as a result of a corporate sale, merger or other business combination or, as is often the case, it may become necessary to set a figure for federal or state income, gift or estate taxes.

The central inquiry, of course, is value. A closely held corporation is a company whose stock is neither listed on any stock exchange nor traded over-the-counter. Accordingly, there is no existing market price for the stock and it therefore becomes necessary to arrive at its value by considering all of the relevant valuation factors. This can be a formidable task, particularly if the company is a large one and has been in existance over a long period of time. Consideration must be given to all relevant factors which may touch upon the value, including a thorough analysis of the financial statements, company reports, forecasts, corporate charter and minutes, management and management agreements, and other important corporate contracts, together with numerous other items.

Although there are a great number of factors to consider in each individual case depending upon the type of corporation and the nature and extent of its business, the normal operating company that deals in the manufacture and sale of products has certain fundamental areas around which the final valuation of its shares will be determined. These areas are the sticks and can be listed as follows:

1. Nature and history of the business
2. Management
3. Sales
4. Operating earnings
5. Other financial data
6. Goodwill
7. Past sales of company stock
8. Percent of interest being valued
9. Stock prices of comparable companies

Note that even in the most complex corporate situation, there can be as few as nine sticks. All of the factual information that the negotiator reviews and retains should be relevant to one of the foregoing sticks. If it is not, it should be eliminated from further consideration.

## Additional Refinement

Here's how a summary of relevant factual material might look under several of the sticks and, further, how by this process of elimination the negotiator can actually fix firmly into his mind the supporting data and negotiate with nothing more than a brief review before each negotiating session.

|                                           | *Summary of factual* |
| *Sticks (fundamental areas)*              | *data relevant to*   |
|                                           | *each stick*         |

1. Nature and history of the business— Nature of products
   —Years in business
   —Markets
   —Growth prospects
   —Competition

2. Management — — —— — — — — —Key men
   —Depth
   —Experience
   —Incentive and training
      programs

4. Operating earnings — — — — — —Last five yrs. net income
      (after elimination of
      non-recurring items)
   —Per share earnings
   —Price/earnings ratio
   —Capitalization of earnings
      rate

5. Other financial data — — — — — —Fixed assets
   —Dividend paying capacity
      (after adjustment for any
      excessive salaries or other
      expenses)
   —Current ratio
   —Book value of stock
   —Corporate debt
   —Price/book value ratio
   —Price/dividend ratio
   —Net working capital
      per share
   —Profit and pension plans

7. Past sales of the company's stock  —Dates of sales
                                        —Prices per share
                                        —Number of shares sold
                                        —Arm's length transactions

Summarized in the right hand column are only matters that are relevant to each stick. Each has been abbreviated for reference purposes only. The negotiator's files should contain all of the information in support of each summarized matter. For example, in number seven above, his files should contain complete information on the date of each past sale of company stock, the price per share and the number of shares sold. Names and other relevant information of each seller and purchaser should also be included in order to substantiate whether the sales were at arm's length, and therefore more likely to represent what the parties to the transaction felt to be the then fair market value of the stock. By neatly organizing all such supporting material into individual folders with each "stick" as the folder title, the negotiator has thus efficiently marshalled his negotiating evidence. His "brain- attic" is thus free of any excess "lumber" and his "tools" of "a large assortment" and "all in the most perfect order," ready for maximum use whenever and however he may have need for them.

# 8

# *Priority of the Five Negotiating Senses*

Most of us learned at a very early age in our formal education that we possess five senses. By experience we have accustomed ourselves to using these senses and have come to take them for granted in our everyday manner of living. We see, hear, touch, smell and taste a variety of things daily. In addition, our senses may assist us in facilitating a trouble-free existance and guard us against known and unknown hazards. Little do many of us realize, however, that there exists a definite priority of the use of these senses. To illustrate, if you would close your eyes and place a finger on a red-hot griddle, the resulting pain would force you to withdraw it quickly. If you opened your eyes, however, and saw the red-hot griddle before even attempting to touch it, the danger would immediately become known and you could thus avert a badly burned finger. Similarly, if you heard the hot griddle crackling from the heat even before you saw it, you might even be earlier forewarned of its danger.

In the foregoing situation there exists a definite priority of the senses. The priority is that sense which will best allow you to reach an *ultimate* conclusion on the character or true nature of the matter that is confronting you. Touching the hot griddle allowed you to discover its heated and thus dangerous nature, but at the expense of a burned finger. That was reaching the ultimate conclusion the hard way. Similarly, hearing its crackling may have spared you from a burned finger but did not allow you to conclusively determine its heated nature for several reasons. There

45

might have been several griddles and the sound would probably not allow you to single out the heated and thus dangerous one. Second, the intensity of the heat could not be learned. Griddles sometimes crackle profusely when first turned on, long before they have become hot enough to burn one's finger. The sense with priority, hence, was sight. By seeing the red-hot griddle, you immediately and conclusively learned of its true character.

A similar priority of the senses is present in virtually every situation that involves the human being. It is not, however, identical in every one. On the contrary, each individual situation may call for a different priority. If, for example, a very tasty-appearing piece of pastry was set before you, your sense of sight might lead you to believe that it was quite delicious. Your sense of smell might enforce that belief. The sense that will best allow you to determine conclusively whether the pastry is really delicious and thus the sense with the ultimate priority is, nevertheless, clearly taste. A bite or two is all that's necessary. Similarly, if you heard a loud noise that sounded like gunfire and rushed out only to discover that it was merely an automobile backfiring, you would be affording priority to the sense of sight, as would a spectator at either a sporting event or movie unless, of course, he preferred to listen to the roar of a crowd or the gunfire in a hero's western, and that was his motive for attending.

Negotiation can obviously only be accomplished by communication between the negotiating parties. All communication must be carried on by use of the five senses. The human brain, man's decision-making organism, can be reached only through his sense of sight, hearing, touch, taste or smell.

Generally, in negotiation the senses of hearing and seeing take precedent over the remaining three. This logically follows, since most negotiation consists of either the spoken word or use of the eyes for examination of written matter, or perhaps simply watching the opposing negotiator intently. There are, however, frequent exceptions. The negotiator should, therefore, always make an independent determination in every negotiation as to which of the senses is the priority sense and will thus best allow him to communicate more effectively.

The senses of taste, smell, or even touch can often creep sufficiently into the negotiation picture to take priority away from the primary two. When this occurs, the negotiator must plan his strategy and tactics accordingly. I can recall one instance in particular where the sense of taste clearly took priority. A controversy had developed over the quality of certain food. One side claimed that the food was perfectly normal and of a high quality. The other alleged that it was of an inferior quality. After preliminary discussion it was suggested that a food expert be called in and that the parties accept his judgment. Both sides agreed. Taste samplings by the food expert convinced the parties that the quality standards had been met. By giving priority to the sense of taste, the point had been successfully made; it was worth a thousand words.

In other situations the sense of smell may take a definite priority. For example, assume you're a city official charged with the responsibility of abating public nuisances. Irate citizens of a particular area claim that an offensive odor coming from a certain meat packing plant is ruining their neighborhood and they demand that something be done. The company denies the charges and contends it is in full compliance with local laws. The controversy heats up to the boiling point and there you are, caught in the middle of a highly emotional issue. Can you negotiate out of it? In most cases, yes! But you must first recognize that the key lies in the priority of senses—smell. You can talk a blue streak without any material progress unless you can recognize that priority. Here's how it might be approached.

First, ask both sides to refrain from any further action or public comment until you've had an opportunity to investigate. Then go out to the neighborhood on several occasions (and bring along an aid or two to get their reaction) to sniff the situation first hand. What you're doing is accumulating facts primarily through use of your sense of smell. After you're satisfied that you've accumulated a sufficient test, then call spokesmen for the parties together for a settlement. But *don't* call them into your office. Ask them to meet at an appropriate place *in the neighborhood.* As you talk, you are, in effect, requiring *everyone* present to give priority to their sense of smell. On this basis your chances of reaching a successful agreement should be excellent.

From what I've written, it's clear that in order for the negotiator to effectively communicate and thus to demonstrate the soundness of his negotiating position, it's essential that he carefully distinguishes which of the five senses has taken the coveted position of priority. His negotiation strategy and tactics should be developed in light of and in recognition of that priority.

# 9

# How to Develop a
# Good Negotiating
# Memory

A good negotiating memory will allow the negotiator to remain fully alert during the discussion without the necessity of frequent outside referrals. In addition, it will permit ease and accuracy in recalling facts and other matters which will not only promote smoothness in delivery and thus make him more effective, but also favorably impress his opponent. Finally, it will provide the negotiator with a feeling of confidence and self assurance that's essential to negotiation success.

## Concentration

The first important requirement on the road to a good negotiating memory is complete concentration during both preparation and the actual discussions. This means concentration on both the broad negotiating objectives together with all relevant facts, laws and other details. As I have pointed out in an earlier section (Presence of the Negotiator's Client), the human mind can effectively concentrate on only one subject matter at a time. The negotiator's thoughts, therefore, should always be centered on the business at hand, to the exclusion of all others.

## Diversification

A second important step toward a good negotiating memory is to examine a matter from as many different viewpoints or angles as possible. Try this simple experiment. Find two unfamiliar objects of equal interest. (You should have some interest in the objects in order to attract your attention to them in the first place). Examine one carefully from all angles—front, rear, sides, and even the inside (under the hood and in the trunk, for example, if it's a new car). Simply look at the other from one angle—any angle—but only one. Spend the same amount of time on each. Which do you think will be more apt to stick in your mind?

When you're preparing for a negotiation, examine the pertinent details from all possible angles. If you're negotiating the sale of a large business, for example, this means that, in conjunction with a close analysis of the financial statements, an inspection of all material fixed assets, such as plants and expensive machinery, should be made whenever possible. Or, as an alternative, a qualified individual should fill you in on their complete details. Talk to key management. It'll greatly assist in keeping this important aspect of any business fresh before your mind. If it's an operating business, try to personally observe the most important phases of actual production. It'll bring the financial statements to life as you study them in preparation for the sessions.

Perhaps a more familiar example might be negotiating the sale of a home. It would benefit the negotiator to go through the entire home, room by room. In other words, look at it from all angles. If the master bedroom is unusually large, with a cozy fireplace setting that you want to remember, examine the setting carefully. Lift up the screen; handle the tongs. Step off the dimensions of the room even though you may already have them written down. It'll take only a few minutes, but when it comes time to remember the details of that "fabulous master bedroom" they'll be there right before you, long after the prospective purchaser has seen them and may need his memory refreshed.

Diversification also means thinking over what has been reviewed as often as possible. Fold a piece of paper once and then straighten it. A slight crease will remain. Fold it a second time and the crease will become even more pronounced. Fold it a dozen times and it's creased forever and will bend with little or no effort. Thinking over matters works the same way. Paths will form in the brain just as the crease in the paper, and recalling pertinent details will be just as easy as rebending the paper.

## Association

A third important practice on the road to a good negotiating memory is to make judicious use of association. Everyone is familiar with the practice of tying a piece of string around the finger. This is merely a form of association. The string is supposed to be a reminder of something to be done. This example, however, is much too basic for negotiation. In addition, it necessitates an irrelevant factor, namely, the string itself. Association for negotiation should always be related only to matters that are directly relevant to the negotiation.

If the negotiator wants to remember, for example, the details of an important real estate appraisal, it would be well to study closely photographs of the property or, if time permits, visit the land itself. As he views the property, he should concentrate on the details of the appraisal. Then, when it comes time to recall details of the appraisal, mentally picturing the land should form the necessary associations. The land thus takes the place of and serves the same function as the string on the finger.

One final thought: notice that association is very similar to diversification. Diversification is actually a form of association. The main difference, however, is that diversification covers all matters relevant to the negotiation, whereas association is generally confined to recalling only key or very important ones.

# 10

# *Language of the Negotiator*

This is an essential section simply because it deals with the most common form of communication in negotiation, the spoken word. Good language in negotiation can be as effective and refreshing as a drink of cool, clear spring water to a man who has been marooned on a searing hot desert. Conversely, poor language can sometimes be as harmful as a cup of arsenic. What you say and how you say it *does* make a difference, as in the case of the two priests who were unable to give up smoking cigarettes. One asked for permission from his superior to "smoke while he was praying." Permission was denied. The other asked for permission to "pray while he was smoking." Permission was granted. Let's therefore look at some of the more important aspects of the language of the negotiator.

At the outset, it is essential that the negotiator use common, basic language. The old saying that simple words work best holds true in negotiation. If, for example, you are talking about the loss of property value due to such factors as outdated plumbing or electrical fixtures and other similar causes, isn't it better to simply say it in those terms rather than, perhaps, "curable functional obsolescence?" The former is easy to understand. The latter? Even an expert in the field may need a pause to think.

The use of simple language applies even though the negotiation may be on a very high level and of great importance. Never assume that the more important the negotiation, the more technical and complex the language should be. Actually, the converse is true. I find from my experience that the more complex the negotiation and the more skillful the opponent, the more basic the language and, thus, the more effective the communication.

Using common basic language does not necessarily mean that the negotiator should not strive to accumulate a wide vocabulary. On the contrary, word power is an important part of his arsenal, and he should therefore exercise every opportunity to strengthen it. The rule that I generally follow and the one that I think leads to the best results is that: The negotiator should know the meaning of virtually as many frequently used words of the English language as possible, so that if they are employed by his opponent (the negotiator need not use them) he will not have to go scurrying for a meaning.

A second important point for the negotiator to bear in mind is to be certain his language is spoken clearly so that there is little danger of any misunderstanding. This can save many headaches. Never hesitate to repeat a statement or to ask that one be repeated by an opponent if it's not understood. In conjunction with this, it's important for the negotiator to speak and act naturally in order to be the most persuasive. Artificialness has little or no place in negotiation, and this includes language.

Avoid strange words or general clichés. Strange words simply may not carry the message and may often call for additional explanations. General clichés are too broad to have any substantial impact in most instances. It's one thing, for example, to say, "That would take in the whole ball of wax" and another to say, "That would take into consideration everything that we've concluded to date." In the former, the field is left wide open and thus ripe for misunderstanding. In the latter, it's confined to only previously discussed matters which, if the negotiator feels is necessary, may be repeated in order to avoid misunderstandings.

Describing a thing or situation can often have much more of an impact than merely a general statement. Proper description will bring the matter alive and help the opponent to form a mental picture, and thus see it more clearly. General or technical words seldom do this. For example, if you are an attorney attempting to negotiate the settlement of a personal injury claim, it is one thing to describe the injury as "a large contusion" and another to describe it as "a deeply imbedded bruise of a serious nature." Both mean essentially the same thing, but the latter brings the injury alive. Language is a living thing; it should be approached on that basis.

It is hardly ever wise to speak lightly about matters that are of great importance or seriously about matters that are of little consequence. In everyday living one does not ordinarily jest at a funeral or speak seriously about making a trip to the corner drive-in to pick up a hamburger. The same rules apply to negotiation. Speaking lightly of matters that are of a serious nature is, perhaps, one of the quickest and easiest ways to make an opponent angry and thus stifle negotiation progress, particularly if the matter directly affects him or his position. Similarly, trying to make a minor matter seem important will generally lead to artificialness, a status which is always wise to avoid since it places the negotiator's sincerity directly and needlessly on the line.

A negotiator should be familiar with any basic technical language that may become involved in any negotiation. This may appear to be inconsistent with striving to employ only common language. I am referring here, however, to basic terms that are frequently used in the particular or special area that may then be the subject matter of the negotiation. For example, if you are negotiating with an underwriter to arrive at the price for a potential offering of corporate stock to the public, terms such as "offering price" or "spread" or "bargain stock" should be a part of your vocabulary. Likewise, if a lease is involved in the negotiation, terms such as "lessor" and "lessee" are a necessity. If a mortgage, terms such as "mortgagor" and "mortgagee" should not be strangers. What this amounts to, in substance, is speaking to your opponent on his level. It will favorably impress him and, even more importantly, allow you to converse without interrupting your train of thought.

Try to avoid words or phrases that are susceptable to different meanings. If they must be used, be certain they are defined early in the negotiation so that there are no later misunderstandings. To illustrate, if you are negotiating a lease, terms such as "net lease," or "net, net lease," or even "net, net, net lease" may be misconstrued if not firmly defined. So make it clear at the outset that you are talking about a lease where the tenant is to pay all real estate taxes, assessments, insurance, cost of repairs, and all other expenses of operating and maintaining the property.

Finally, just as I will later point out in the section on correspondence, one word can often be crucial. Double negatives, for example, may not only confuse but also be misconstrued. "I don't have no offers" may mean that I do have some, since if I don't have none, I must have some. So drop the "don't" and simply say, "I have no offers." This is merely an example and should amply illustrate the need for proper language, particularly if the negotiation is one of great importance. In fact, as I've already indicated, the greater the importance, the greater the need for good language. Never lose sight of the fact, however, that practicing good language on little matters as well as the large will greatly reduce the chances of error in every case!

# 11

# *The Need for Objectivity*

A skillful negotiator must look at every issue coolly and objectively, with icy veins that refuse to warm up until he has cut through the formalities, brushed aside any bias, and examined the matter in its true light. He simply cannot afford the luxury of permitting personalities to influence either his analysis of a matter or his efforts at the bargaining table. Nor can he permit his own emotions to cloud his judgment. Only in this manner can he ever hope to exercise the kind of judgment that is indispensable to successful negotiation. One of Abraham Lincoln's greatest strengths was his complete objectivity in selecting people to whom he entrusted responsibility. He disregarded his own personal like or dislike for them. The sole inquiry was always: Can he contribute to the advancement of the Nation's goals? It's no wonder Lincoln was one of the greatest leaders in the history of the entire world. With that type of objectivity he had a lot going for him.

Often, during the course of preparation for the negotiation of large matters, I literally sit in the chair to be occupied by my opponent and mentally run through every one of my proposals in order to eliminate any flaws that may cause an unravelling, as yarn in a knitted sweater will sometimes do. This type of objectivity is necessary and helps the negotiator to see the overall picture more accurately, and thus considerably strengthens his hand during the discussions.

If the negotiator has negotiated with an opponent before, he can, of course, take into consideration his opponent's strengths and weaknesses. But he should also look at him very objectively, not taking him for granted. For he may have eliminated weaknesses and increased his strengths, or maybe even acquired more weaknesses. Whatever the case, a fresh, objective look at him will best enable the negotiator to quickly discover this very early in the discussions.

In long, drawn out negotiations that require frequent contact between the negotiating parties, the danger of losing one's objectivity normally increases simply because of the frequent contact. A negotiator should, therefore, always *periodically* take a fresh look at all matters as they then stand in order to be certain that he is still looking at the same clear picture that was there prior to the time the discussions commenced. This includes not only the subject matter of the negotiation and his positions, but also his opponent.

One final thought on the need for objectivity. There is a very fine line between freedom from personal feelings in one's judgment and bias. I therefore suggest that the negotiator "sit in his opponent's chair" whenever he has any suspicion that his decisions may have become tainted.

# 12

# Pre-Negotiation Organization

At the date of this writing I am engaged in the negotiation of a very large matter that has in excess of fifty negotiable issues. If I were to stack my files one on top of the other, they would perhaps measure three feet or more. Yet, if I am to be effective at the bargaining sessions, it is essential that I have immediate access to every document in that pile. "Instant reference" is how I like to refer to it. And the only feasible way to get it is by concise pre-negotiation organization.

I think that perhaps the need for complete organization prior to entering any negotiation can best be expressed by comparing it to the organizational efforts that the members of a football team must go through prior to the successful execution of any play in Saturday or Sunday's big game. Their actions must be so well organized that there is no danger of missed blocks, men running into each other or standing with no place to go. On the contrary, the exact assignment for each man is mapped out in a plan of operation that tells him where to go and what to do. The whole unit thus functions as a team. All of this is done within the framework of a specific plan and schedule, for both the team and their coach know that they can never expect to put the ball across the opponent's goal line in any other manner.

The same need for systematic organization is present in every negotiation. The exact amount varies with each individual negotiator and negotiation. Some may take little work, particularly if the negotiator is experienced and has negotiated similar matters before. Others, however, that may be highly complex and important, may require much more organizational effort. Whichever the case, the task must be undertaken. Here, therefore, are some pointers to assist in this important aspect of any negotiation.

I always find it helpful to place all supporting data for each issue or groups of related issues in individual folders. In addition, as I have already pointed out in the "Stick Theory" of preparation, these folders may be set up with each stick representing a separate folder title. In this manner it is much easier to locate all of the related information on each particular issue. This may become extremely important during the course of any discussion when reference is made to particular issues at random. No need for the negotiator to attempt to speculate on the answer or fumble around trying to locate the file. By going to the individual folder (which, of course, is appropriately labeled) he has at his fingertips any information that he may need.

Another practice that I have found to be excellent is to utilize different colored inks. This may be very helpful in locating specific paragraphs, words or other information within a particular file. Green ink, for example, may represent highly important matters that the negotiator may want to be certain not to overlook during the discussions; blue ink for names, places, or other specific matters; other colors, of course, can likewise be wisely employed. One word of caution here. I have found from my experience that red ink should generally be avoided. In our everyday activities, red normally signifies danger in one degree or another. From the actual red light that we see on the street corners to the imaginary red ink on the balance sheet of a company that is losing money, red ink, or the thought of it, may tend to make an opponent misconstrue its significance. It's human nature. (Remember that, as you negotiate, your papers may sometimes be set before you, not to be read by the opposition but perhaps for him to glance at.) Seeing red ink marks on them may, therefore, inadvertently prove detrimental.

Placing all correspondence in chronological order with the last letter on top is an excellent method of organizing for easy reference. In fact, I've found one of the quickest and perhaps best ways to learn precisely what has transpired on any situation or transaction is to review correspondence that is set up in this manner. One that I can recall in particular paid great dividends. Certain services were performed by a party pursuant to what the party performing the services alleged was in accordance with a contract. My client was wholly dissatisfied with the services and maintained that no contract existed, and that the services were to be performed on a conditional basis, subject to approval. A pile of disorganized correspondence running over a fairly long period of time was thrust upon my desk. Others had reviewed it, but without any apparent success. I quickly arranged it in chronological order and read it through. Everything seemed to indicate that a contract existed except for one sentence in a single letter which supported our position. This language was called to the attention of the party that performed the services, and the matter was quickly and favorably settled.

Pictures and other graphic data should be kept apart from other written data for easy reference. The same applies to physical exhibits such as mechanical apparatus and blackboards. Keep them handy, but preferably out of sight so that they don't detract from your presentation. Otherwise, an opponent may dwell upon them while you're talking and you may lose some of your effectiveness. Clarence Darrow, one of the outstanding trial lawyers of his time, reportedly utilized a similar technique during a trial. He would push a thin, strong piece of wire through a long cigar (smoking was permitted in some of the court rooms). During the course of his opponent's final argument to the jury, Darrow would light the cigar and, pretending to be in deep thought, hold it up between his fingers for the jury to see. The jury's eyes (and their attention) soon became glued to it during the course of the entire final argument, waiting for the ash to drop off as it grew longer and longer. When the opponent's final argument was completed, little, if any, was actually heard. The jury's attention had been claimed by that unbelievably long, gray ash.

If the negotiator is going to make reference in the negotiation to textbooks, magazines or other bound literature, he should be certain that the appropriate pages or chapters are adequately marked for easy reference. In addition, cross references to the pages should be kept in his notes in the event a marker inadvertently drops out. Thus, he can easily refer to the pages without breaking his train of thought or making it appear as if he's not well organized.

Finally, it's important for the negotiator not to over-organize. He should learn to judge his own capabilities and tailor his organizational efforts to fit them. This means that his materials should be organized so that there are as few reference sources as possible, since he doesn't want to become mentally bogged down with them and thus deprive himself of concentration on the substance of the issues. In addition, his organizational efforts should be confined to materials that are relevant to the issues. Similarly, the negotiator should realize that he must organize himself to fit the negotiation he is about to undertake. Otherwise, pre-negotiation organization doesn't become a useful tool to assist him in constructing and advocating his positions, but it becomes a jungle of references and cross-references which he must cut through at every step or turn.

# 13

# Selection and Use of Assistants

In many instances a negotiator will be able to employ the talents of one or more assistants. They can be a tremendous asset in many respects and, if properly directed, will greatly facilitate matters such as those that require large amounts of research or investigation. On the other hand, there is always some degree of risk involved, particularly if they are going to be present during the bargaining.

## Some Thoughts on Selection

The ideal assistant should be something as follows, bearing in mind that to achieve perfection in anything in life is virtually an impossibility.

- —He should be a person of good character and ability. I place the requirement of character first. What good is ability without character?
- —He should be able to follow instructions to the letter, even though they may sometimes seem absurd and he feels that he has a better idea.
- —He should be tight-lipped and speak only when spoken to, and then only after due deliberation.
- —He should enjoy working more than playing. In fact, his work should be his play. Successful negotiation often entails enormous amounts of plain, hard work.
- —His appearance should be neat and reserved, particularly if

he is going to sit in on the discussions. Flashing color combinations and long, unkept hair, for example, have no place in most negotiations.

—He should be objective in his analysis of every aspect of the negotiation and never be satisfied with his depth of probing.

—He should be of the curious breed. Long hours of research and preparation should only serve to stimulate his imagination and whet his appetite for more. I am always encouraged by an assistant who comes into the office fully prepared to discuss any aspect of a negotiation and more often than not has answers to most of the questions raised.

—Lastly, he should be a perfectionist. Words such as "I think" should be replaced by "Yes, here's the answer," or "I don't know but I'll find out." That's the type of effort that's essential to negotiation success.

Does he sound too good to be true? Of course he does! But those are the guidelines that I would encourage any negotiator to look for. If he can latch on to an assistant with only fifty per cent of them, he's got a real find. Pay him well and guard him well. If only thirty-three percent, take him—good men are hard to find!

## Use of Assistants

After you've been fortunate enough to locate the ideal assistant, here's how I would encourage you to employ him.

Strictly speaking, it's best to have an assistant participate in every aspect of the preparation in order for him to know precisely what is going on and to enable him to gain experience. In addition, he is less apt to be curious and thus less likely to interrupt if he's present at the negotiation.

Skillful opponents sometimes like to ask assistants questions or direct discussions toward them in order to get them to reply or perhaps merely nod in agreement. This has a tendency to indirectly commit the negotiator. At other times an assistant may get the urge to join in, particularly if he feels an opponent is vulnerable, little realizing that skillful opponents sometimes like to make themselves appear helpless in order to "invite" someone to come to their rescue. The urge to respond sometimes becomes so great that an assistant may begin fidgeting nervously in his chair like a boiler about to blow. What generally flows when the lid comes off is often sprinkled liberally with emotion, and not clear and objective deliberation. Moreover, and as I have already related, the art of negotiation necessitates that a negotiator be able to demonstrate the merits of his position under any conceivable circumstances and in any given situation. This literally means that often his strategy and the techniques he adopts must be created "instantly," as the discussions dictate. He's thus not in a position to keep an assistant fully informed, and the latter may become puzzled rather easily. For all of these reasons, I, therefore, always caution any assistant to remain silent during the course of any negotiation unless *I* either ask him a question or give him instructions to the contrary. You can, therefore, see the need for a well-disciplined individual who will not only keep his peace but also not divulge his intentions by untimely facial expressions or other revealing mannerisms. Damaging remarks by an opponent, for example, should merit, if anything, nothing more than a passive glance, and if an assistant feels compelled to answer an opponent's question, he should tactfully defer to the negotiator.

From what I've just related, it should be apparent that decisions during the course of any negotiation must be made by the negotiator, without counsel or advice from assistants unless requested. Joint decision-making authority often results in either no decisions at all or very poor ones. An experienced and skillful negotiator soon comes to the realization that positive decisions must be made by only one person who has both the responsibility and the authority to make them.

In closing this section, there is one additional point that is worthy of mention. Never fail to introduce any assistants prior to the commencement of the negotiation. It's a common courtesy and a necessity to them, and will also obviate any unnecessary apprehension or suspicion on the opponent's part as to who these intelligent, good-looking, impeccably dressed individuals are with the deadpan faces who never seem to lose their cool.

# 14

# Knowledge of Procedure

Assume that you're going to take an automobile trip to a remote corner of the country. Along the way you will obviously encounter a great number of crossroads. Some will have signs to serve as guidelines. Others, particularly as you leave the major thoroughfares, will have none, and if you have to depend upon either peering down each long road or asking others, you might become hopelessly lost rather easily. The solution, of course, is to have a well-laid-out road map that pinpoints every nook and cranny along the way.

To possess an expert knowledge of procedure in any negotiation is to have such a road map. Perhaps this section is orientated more toward the professional because I can think of no greater area where knowledge of procedure is more vital than in the law. And as our laws become even more voluminous and complex, the need for the lawyer-negotiator to possess an expertise in such knowledge magnifies itself immensely.

Take, for example, the federal tax area. Assume that the revenue agent who is auditing the taxpayer's tax return and the taxpayer or his representative have come to a disagreement on the correct amount of tax due. (Sound familiar?) That means that the taxpayer has now reached an important crossroad and a decision must be made as to which direction to go. Shall he ask for a conference at the District Director's level, or bypass that level and seek a conference at the Appellant level? Or perhaps he should bypass both and request that a Notice of Deficiency (often referred to as the "90 Day Letter") be issued by the government, setting forth the amount of tax due so that he can go directly to the Tax Court and thereafter attempt to negotiate. Maybe he can get more favorable treatment with Justice Department attorneys and should therefore pay the tax, and after his claim for a refund has been denied (as it generally is), go to a federal district court for relief.

As you can see, the options are already considerable and he hasn't even exhausted all of the possibilities. Moreover, it may be necessary in some circumstances to go into even greater detail and consider the procedures that the negotiator's opponent must resort to. It may be important for the negotiator to know, for example, at what level of the Revenue Service the Notice of Deficiency is prepared, since it may heavily influence the procedural route he chooses to follow in attempting to demonstrate that the Government's determination of a tax deficiency is erroneous. I can think of an instance, for example, where a favorable decision on this critical aspect of procedure later proved vital to a very successful negotiation outcome.

To take another important instance, when negotiating a matter, the solution to which centers around the validity of a corporate action, it's axiomatic that the negotiator know the respective rights and liabilities of the various classes of stock; what notices are involved, if any, to hold a general or special meeting, and the number of shares of each class necessary to constitute a quorum and thus to legally transact business. The same applies to directors. Answers to such questions as: "What constitutes a quorum?" "How is a vacancy filled?" and, "Is a director who receives notice of a meeting but doesn't attend bound by all actions taken at the meeting?" are all locked up in one form or another in corporate procedure, and should be no strangers to the negotiator if he expects to successfully reach his destination. This means, of course, that he must have a concise knowledge of the applicable state corporation laws since a corporation is a creation of statute, the corporate charter together with the by-laws. It also means that he must have the practical ability to apply this knowledge whenever necessary during the negotiations.

Never lose sight of the fact that a procedure is nothing more than a way of doing something. I have negotiated numerous matters, many of great importance, where the procedure followed played an important part in the final successful outcome. I've already alluded to one in the federal tax area. I pay great attention to procedure—I work hard to know it thoroughly in every negotiation, weaving it into the issues involved and always carefully employing it to my advantage. An expert knowledge of it helps me to select the proper direction at each crossroad, regardless of whether the number of roads is large or small. Lack of knowledge of it, as I've already indicated, can get one hopelessly lost rather easily, like when my platoon sergeant misread his map and had us digging in on a position about to be attacked by our own troops. Fortunately the error was discovered in time, although it almost cost him his stripes. If he would have been a negotiator it might have cost him the negotiation.

# 15

# *The Importance of Maintaining Negotiating Bases*

In every negotiable issue there exists both a primary base and one or more secondary bases. The primary base is the negotiator's ultimate objective on that particular issue. His secondary bases are those *positive* factors which are relevant to the issue being negotiated and which support the primary base. During the course of his preparation, it's the negotiator's task to find these bases, isolate them, and maintain them in the forefront of his thoughts throughout the entire negotiation. At first glance this may appear to be a very elementary matter. Yet, during the heat of the discussion, when pressures have mounted and decisions which may have long-range effects must be made quickly, intelligently and accurately, it can become a very formidable task. In fact, experience has shown that failure of the negotiator to maintain his negotiating bases is a fairly common occurrence, and one of the most costly errors in terms of negotiating results.

## The Primary Base

During the course of a negotiation which ran continuously over a period of seven or eight hours, one of the issues centered around a clause in a contract which granted my client the option to repurchase a certain asset after a period of years had elapsed

68

from the effective date of the agreement. Counsel for the other side wanted the provision out, since his client was very reluctant to let go of an asset that he felt would be quite profitable. My client, on the other hand, wanted the option provision to remain, because much of his future planning centered around it. I, therefore, remained firm. My opponent objected strenuously. I asked the reason for his objection, and he related that the valuation formula in the option clause did not take into consideration any goodwill after the expiration of the period of years.

I said, "Let's add it in."

He then altered his tactics by contending that the formula did not specify the exact number of years prior to the option date that must be considered in arriving at the value of the asset.

I said, "Let's add it in."

He then countered with the proposition that the language did not provide that all relevant valuation factors should be considered in arriving at the buy-back price.

I said, "Let's add it in."

He agreed.

From the foregoing, it's readily apparent that my ultimate objective on the particular issue being negotiated was the necessity of my client to have the option clause remain in the contract. It formed the bottom of the pyramid on which all of the facts, law, and other relevant data rested. It was, in short, my primary base. If I had allowed it to escape from the forefront of my thoughts, my client's option clause would have come tumbling out of the contract and my efforts on his behalf would have thus failed.

Losing sight of one's primary base, as earlier related, is a fairly common everyday occurrence. Take the man who drives his car into a service station to get a quart of oil and winds up with a complete oil change; or the lady who sets out to buy a hat or handbag and inevitably brings home, instead, an entire wardrobe, much to her husband's chagrin, or the man who goes into the sporting goods store to buy a box of shotgun shells and comes out the proud owner of a new shotgun. All have one thing in common—a lost objective.

That's precisely what happened to my opponent. Every point raised by him and agreed upon by me were valuation factors normally considered in arriving at the value of the asset in question. They, therefore, added nothing of substance to the broadly worded option clause and thus did not detract even the slightest from my primary base. Because I readily agreed to each of them without hesitation, my opponent became confused and allowed the option clause to remain in the contract.

## Secondary Bases

To simply illustrate secondary bases and their use, let's take our friend who went in to get the quart of oil. The positive factors in his favor are quite plain. He has a car with room for a quart of oil, and he presumably has the cash to pay for it. In addition, there is another station across the street (there always is) that would welcome his business.

"I'd like a quart of your best oil, please" he says.

Does the station attendant say, "Yes sir! I'll get it right away." No! He's very enterprising and immediately sets out to negotiate a larger sale. He tells our car-owning friend, "Oil changes are on special this week if you fill your tank up with gas and also get our regular grease job. It's a real saving," he continues, "and the offer expires in two days." (It always seems to expire in a very short time. This adds to our car-owning friend's anxiety). "It's a real bargain," he says, again throwing in the clincher.

"I . . . don't have that much time," replies the car owner, caught somewhat off guard.

"It won't take long," counters the operator. "There's no one ahead of you. We'll have you out of here in fifteen minutes. Maybe even sooner!"

"Well . . . I . . . didn't bring that much cash. I . . . "

"No problem," interrupts the attendant. "You can use your credit card (everyone, of course, has one of these, too) or you can open a charge account."

We all know what usually happens. By now our poor car-owning friend's friendly grin has turned to a grimace. His primary base has gone completely down the drain. A quart of oil has now expanded into a complete oil change, grease job, and a full tank of gas. His secondary bases? He lost sight of them as soon as the attendant hit him with that pitch on the special. Initially, he held all of the trump cards. He probably should have said, "No, thank you. All the old buggy needs is a quart of your best oil.

How much is it?" Combining this with a quick but obvious glance at the station across the street would have probably gotten him his quart of oil forthwith. With that simple response and gesture he would have very effectively used all of his secondary bases to quickly attain his primary one. By taking the defensive, however, they completely escaped him, and he became easy prey for the enterprising attendant.

Now let's look closely at another illustration, one that is perhaps a bit more conducive to formal negotiation but still staying within a fairly common daily occurrence. Assume that Smith and Jones are to get together to negotiate the sale of a parcel of real estate on which an office building will be constructed. Smith is the seller and Jones is the purchaser. Assume, further, that Smith would like to get five hundred thousand dollars for the property, whereas Jones would like to acquire the property for only three hundred thousand. Both Smith and Jones have thoroughly analyzed the facts pertaining to the property. Smith knows, among other things, that the property is a prime location for an office building; that it is basically level and would, therefore, not require extensive grading, which can be very costly; that complete shopping facilities are within walking distance; that it is conveniently located near air transportation; and, finally, that there is another buyer interested in the property.

Jones, on the other hand, has found that past soil tests indicate that additional costs will have to be incurred in constructing the foundation; that local zoning regulations restrict the building's height; that ingress and egress to and from the property are difficult; and, finally, that Smith turned down another recent offer on the property for four hundred thousand dollars but that this earlier offer was on a contractual basis payable over a five year period, whereas Smith wanted cash to offset other capital losses and for use for other pending investments.

At the outset, it is well to note that I have listed only the key or most important positive valuation factors relevant to each side. Obviously, there exist numerous others which must be taken into consideration in arriving at a final sale price. For our purposes, however, these should suffice.

Smith's or Jones' primary base is, of course, to complete the sale on the basis most favorable to them. Their secondary bases are the above listed factors which are favorable to each. If either is to prevail, he must demonstrate to the other that his own secondary bases are the most dominating. If neither is able to do so, then there will either be no suitable agreement reached or the matter will be seriously compromised.

If, during the course of the discussion, Smith raises the fact that the property is primely located and near shopping and transportation, Jones may counter with the unfavorable zoning and poor ingress and egress. If Jones raises the need for additional foundation costs because of what the soil tests disclosed, Smith can counter by pointing out that no substantial grading costs need be incurred. And if Smith should try to win the day by relating, "Why should I accept your offer when I have already turned down one for four hundred thousand dollars, and I have another potential buyer?" Jones, of course, may point out that his offer is for cash, which can be put to immediate use. This jockeying back and forth forms the basis of any negotiation.

In this example I have fairly equalized the secondary bases. Often, however, they can and do rest heavily in favor of one side or the other. When this occurs, the side with the greatest number should ordinarily prevail, all other things being equal. In actual practice, however, this is seldom the case due to numerous factors, such as the respective skills of the negotiators together with many, many others, the least of which is not failure of the negotiator to maintain his secondary bases.

One final thought—I have found that the failure to maintain bases is directly proportionate to the complexity of the issues being negotiated. The negotiator who is confronted with numerous and entangled issues and also faced with discussions that may drag out over a considerable period of time should, therefore, take great pains to keep his bases impressed firmly within his mind. By skillfully employing them he may thus be afforded the opportunity to swing the negotiating pendulum unalterably in his favor.

# 16
# Habit (Friend or Foe)

In order to fully comprehend the forceful part that habit plays in our daily lives, we need only reflect upon our activities from the time we climb out of bed in the morning until we retire at night. Simple acts such as tying our shoes, combing our hair, and brushing our teeth are all made automatic because of habit. Its forceful effect can also be found in the letters that we write, our speech, and even the clothes that we wear. All of these and many, many more are done with virtually little or no conscious mental effort.

Why, then, are good habits so important to a negotiator? They are important simply because they will free his mind for precious concentration on other essential matters. Moreover, good habits will favorably reflect upon his report and personal stature, thereby facilitating his effectiveness at the bargaining table. Conversely, developing or continuing bad habits can only serve to work against him, and their harmful effect can crop up at virtually every twist and turn in the bargaining.

## Common Bad Habits That Should Be Avoided

Blinking nervously, particularly when discussing important issues, seems to be fairly common in negotiation. I once negotiated with an opponent with this nervous habit, which became even more pronounced when he was about to make a proposal that he knew would not be accepted. It was a tip-off to his intentions.

Speaking before an opponent has fully stated his position is another common bad habit that should be avoided unless intentional on the negotiator's part. The Bible put it another way: "He that answereth a matter before he heareth *it*, it *is* folly and shame unto him."[2] One of the harmful aspects of this bad habit is that the person possessing it seldom consciously reflects upon the statements he is interrupting and thus does not consider whether they possess any hidden motives. Hence, when this habit is acute, a skillful negotiator may guide the one with the habit into finishing sentences in a manner most favorable to him, or perhaps even into supplying information that might otherwise not be available. To illustrate, assume you're negotiating the sale of an antique and you want to determine whether the potential purchaser wants it for himself or is representing another. (People of means frequently have others buy for them in order to keep the price down.) You notice during the course of the discussions that your opponent tends to break in before you've finished speaking. Here's how you might gain the information you want by taking advantage of his bad habit:

Negotiator: "This antique will go well in an elegant dining room with an expensive chandelier hanging overhead; don't you agree that if ... "

Opponent (interrupting): "Yes, it certainly will; no doubt about it. And I think my price is reasonable."

Negotiator: "An easy item to resell, if a person want ... "

Opponent: "I don't intend to resell it."

Negotiator: "It's for you then and ... "

Opponent (avoiding a direct response): "The price is right, that's the important thing."

(Taking your opponent at his word, you have quickly learned by taking advantage of his bad habit that the antique is not being purchased for resale and that he's evasive and noncommital on whether he's buying for himself. The examples, of course, are endless, but the foregoing amply illustrates how an opponent's bad habit of interrupting can work to the negotiator's advantage.)

Constant fidgeting in the chair or use of outside or foreign objects is commonplace. For example, frequently lighting cigarettes or moving pencils around tends to distract an opponent's attention from the negotiator's presentation. I can recall one

---

[2] PROVERBS 18:13

instance in particular when an opponent repeatedly opened and closed the latch of his briefcase as he spoke. It interfered considerably with both my concentration and his effectiveness.

Using similar words too often is also commonplace. For example, "I . . . ah . . . ah . . . feet . . . ah . . . ah . . . that . : . ah . . . our thinking is . . . ah . . . . " The "ah's," or whatever the repetitious word or words may be, are sometimes repeated so often that it becomes difficult to follow the substance of what is being said or, for that matter, to concentrate at all. I once negotiated a matter with an opponent who would constantly (and because it was so habitual, unknowingly) pause between words or phrases and let out with a nervous "umph!" It worked greatly to his detriment.

Looking away from an opponent when talking to him is another recurring bad habit that should be avoided. It can have particularly harmful effects when discussing important matters because it may tend to reflect upon the negotiator's sincerity.

Finally, reading from or jotting down notes on papers, pads, clipboards or similar items that are conspicuously held up so that the opponent cannot see them is another very harmful bad habit that should be avoided. In fact, it can be downright disastrous! It tends to make an opponent very suspicious and thus unnecessarily places a question mark directly upon the negotiator's credibility. The opponent usually feels that he is somehow being taken advantage of or that matters he should know about are deliberately being withheld from him. He becomes uncertain of himself and "clams up" considerably, or even becomes reluctant to continue the negotiation.

## How to Develop Good Habits and Break Bad Ones

The best way to develop good habits is to practice them on virtually everything the negotiator does. Habits are nothing more than pathways through the brain. Every time one performs an act a pathway is formed. The more the same act is performed the deeper the pathway becomes, sort of like the path across the neighbor's yard or the vacant lot that served as a shortcut when we were kids. The more it was used, the deeper became the rut.

Practicing good eye contact, for example, with everybody we meet will eventually lead to good eye contact in negotiation.

Similarly, speaking clearly on every occasion will eventually lead to a flawless delivery in even the toughest negotiations. Conversely, of course, one can never carry bad habits around with him everywhere he goes and expect them to suddenly disappear when it comes time to negotiate. The paths are generally too deep.

As far as breaking bad habits is concerned, the first essential point is to learn to recognize them. I've listed above some of the more common. My list, however, only scratches the surface. They come in all sizes and varieties, and some may be peculiar to one individual and not another. A short person, for example, might tend to sit too rigidly in order to bring himself up to eye level, whereas a taller person may tend to slouch. These are physical habits. Both are obviously very poor. It would be better for the short man to get an adjustable chair to control his height, or perhaps even a chair pad. The taller man can lower himself if he desires although, as I have already pointed out, looking down at an opponent can be a definite asset.

After the bad habits have been weeded out, the best way to break them is to do so decisively. Once an action becomes habitual, it becomes pleasant. This includes bad habits. That's one reason why persons with bad habits find them sometimes extremely difficult to break. Gradual cessation in an attempt to break them is usually ineffective and normally results in a temporary cutting down, but the idea is to eliminate them entirely. A bad habit to any degree may prove just as harmful. If, for example, you look away from your opponent on just one important occasion, it may be enough to make you pay the price. You don't want to repeat the act any longer because it will deepen the path. So the break must therefore be decisive and complete.

In conjunction with a decisive break, it's sometimes very helpful to undertake actions that are directly opposite to the bad habit. If the bad habit, for example, is chronic tardiness, making an effort to be *early* at every opportunity rather than just on time will form a new and more desirable path rather quickly, and soon the bad habit will be replaced by a good one. Of course, at first this will take conscious effort. But after the action has been repeated often enough, it will soon become automatic.

# 17

# *The Use of Correspondence in Negotiation*

Correspondence is an essential part of any negotiation and should be afforded a position of high priority. Its uses are numerous and should be fully recognized by the negotiator. Never assume that negotiation is confined to oral discussion. That may be a costly error. I have participated in negotiations where my opponent handled himself very well at the bargaining table, only to fumble the ball badly with his correspondence.

### Correspondence Can Be An Effective Control Device

To illustrate, assume that negotiations have been carried on by various negotiators of a corporation over a period of time to sell or merge the business. The other side becomes very indignant when discussions are broken off and sends an angry letter threatening legal action, claiming that a completed agreement for the sale or merger existed. If the letter is limited to a threat, as may often be the case, it would be unwise in most instances to respond by raising any new matters other than those that may have been already pointed out as reasons for breaking off the discussions. By staying within the reasons cited and reiterating them in writing, you are effectively keeping the matter within existing boundaries.

In the foregoing illustration, if the threatening letter is more specific and perhaps even raises new matters, your answer should fully respond to only those that are material and relevant, in addition to restating your earlier reasons for not pursuing the negotiation. Never allow needless wandering into other areas. New matters raised that are not pertinent should likewise be responded to, but only so far as is necessary to point out why they are of no consequence. This will prevent the other side from misconstruing silence on them as an admission of their importance.

Whenever an angry, insulting, or threatening letter is received, there is always the temptation to fight fire with fire. That will only serve to broaden the flame and perhaps even provide enough fuel to allow it to burn completely out of control. In such circumstances, always remain calm and objective, particularly if your client is the one who received the letter and is angry. If he's unable to retain his anger, ask him to let you take care of it and you'll keep him fully advised. He'll appreciate it.

I always like to begin my answer to such letters something like this: "Thank you for your letter of the 21st," or whatever the date happens to be. This tends to immediately cool off the situation. Following it with a terse but objective analysis of the pertinent facts and other relevant matters will generally assist in bringing the entire picture back into its proper perspective.

## Correspondence Can Be Used to Deemphasize

Often in a negotiation a matter may balloon completely out of proportion. "Making a mountain out of a molehill," I believe, is the most familiar cliché. Correspondence may be the perfect vehicle to bring it back down to earth. The mere act of stating in writing that the matter is not of great importance (and why) will often prove helpful. There is something about the printed word that lends credibility. People are more apt to believe what they see than what they hear.

Placing a matter in parentheses may decrease its importance, as may inserting it at the end of a letter or memorandum after the signature as a postscript. Also, language such as, "We place little emphasis on . . . " or "I see little merit in . . . " is a good way to deemphasize.

## Correspondence Can Be Used to Clarify or Restate Positions

Following up oral discussions with a letter or memorandum setting forth the pertinent details is an excellent way to avoid misunderstandings. Often, when a negotiation is complicated or drawn out over a period of time, or when numerous parties are involved, details can be interpreted differently, or perhaps even lost or forgotten. Backtracking can consume valuable time and energy, and is costly. In those situations where the negotiator considers it necessary, he should therefore follow up the discussion with some form of written correspondence.

## Who Should Receive Copies

Normally all parties to a transaction should receive copies of any significant correspondence relative to it. There are, however, certain situations where this may not be advisable. To illustrate, sometimes the author of a threatening letter has made a mistake and is attempting to gloss over it by taking a demanding position. If he is representing others and has sent copies of his letter to them, he may not have apprised them of his error. It might be wiser in such circumstances to confine your reply to only the author, particularly if you wish to point out where the errors were made. He'll generally get the point and encourage his people not to press the matter. If you take the latter approach and send copies of your letter to those who received copies of his, you may be running the risk of embarrassing him and thus plunging him more fervently into the matter. Remember, you're interested in results, not publishing the errors of others. Your opponent will appreciate your consideration for not "advertising" his error and recognizing that he's human, too. Good judgment is necessary here, and each case must turn upon its own facts.

Another area where it may not be wise to send copies to all other participants is the reverse of the above. In this situation, the opponent's clients may be aggressively pursuing a position that is either unfounded or unreasonable. Sending copies of correspondence to them may merely make them more determined. A wiser course might be to send correspondence to only their representative (even if he's already sent copies of his demanding letter to his clients), pointing out clearly why his client's position is not well founded. He'll quickly get the picture and may thus become your virtual ally, and work to pursuade them to drop the matter.

## Other Helpful Thoughts on Correspondence

A negotiator should always strive to look good on paper. That means that his stationery should be neat, printed if possible, and never gaudy. His correspondence is an integral part of his image, and his opponent will form impressions from what he sees on paper. Neatness is therefore a must. Printed letterheads are relatively inexpensive and will pay for themselves over and over again. Typed letters are best unless the matter to be negotiated is very personal. If a handwritten letter is sent, be certain that the writing is legible and no messy smudges, fingerprints or other distasteful marks are present.

Good grammar and proper punctuation, together with simple, clear sentences, are obviously essential to effective communication and need not be mentioned further here.

Always be certain that the correct amount of postage is used. Nothing can be more embarrassing than to have an important letter arrive with an insufficient postage mark. It's a reflection not only upon the negotiator but also the people working with him.

Be sure that your correspondence is accurate. On important matters I often proofread my letters just to be certain that all technical language is correct. Sometimes one word can make a vast difference. It's one thing to say, "Your position is *not* acceptable," or "We do *not* feel the price is reasonable," and entirely another if the word "not" is inadvertently omitted. It can sometimes be very difficult to explain the error, particularly if the other side has already acted upon the strength of the correspondence.

Be prompt with your correspondence. Procrastination may not only be harmful in terms of time lost, but certainly will pay the negotiator no dividends if his opponent must go through the inconvenience and expense of writing again or perhaps calling on the telephone to find out the cause of the delay.

In conclusion, the reader should recognize that in this section I've attempted to set forth some of the more important functions of correspondence in order to illustrate its significance. Obviously its uses can be endless, but only if the negotiator is fully cognizant of its importance.

# 18

# *Commencement of the Negotiation*

Let's begin this section by considering some basics. Whenever possible the negotiator should be comfortably situated before he begins negotiating. First impressions are vitally important, particularly if the opponent is a new one. Thus, discussions should never commence while the negotiator, for example, has his coat in hand, papers not yet out of his briefcase, or even while he's sipping that first cup of coffee.

It's important to win the respect of the opponent as early as possible. One of the best ways to do this is to convey an impression of calmness and deliberation. In addition, the negotiator will find that making a good initial impression will carry over and make an opponent more receptive throughout the entire negotiation.

The moment a negotiator greets his opponent is actually the time to begin being observant. As I will point out in a later section, the negotiator's concentration should be fixed on his opponent while the drama is unfolding in front of him. Sometimes the blinking of an opponent's eyes can have significance, as can the way he turns down the corners of his mouth or tightly grips his pencil.

If the negotiator hasn't ascertained the precise character of the negotiation prior to the commencement, it's important for him to do so as early as possible in order to develop his strategy and techniques. Obviously, a negotiation that is highly adverse may call for an entirely different approach than one that's secure and consists of merely arriving at a meeting of the minds on fairly routine issues.

The commencement of a negotiation is a good time for the negotiator to place himself on either a common or higher plane than his opponent. I'm referring here to the negotiator's personal experiences and background. This is a form of personal equalization and is necessary not only to help find some common ground between the parties, but also in order to obviate any danger of an opponent erroneously thinking that there exists weakness on the negotiator's part. This is particularly useful, for example, to a younger negotiator who doesn't want his youth to be misconstrued for lack of experience or ability, as may sometimes be the case, or when dealing with an opponent who has a considerable wealth of experience with the issues to be negotiated. If, for example, the negotiator has previously worked in a capacity similar to his opponent or has negotiated similar matters of equal or greater importance, he should not be reluctant to tactfully and timely point this out to his opponent very early in the discussions.

Finally, and perhaps most importantly, it's essential to begin any negotiation, whether adverse or not, on a friendly and positive vein. This means that controversial matters should be reserved until after the negotiation environment has taken on an air of compatibility. Getting an opponent to say "Yes" should be an early objective. Often this may entail discussions of relatively minor matters, or perhaps even matters that have no direct connection with the issues to be negotiated. The weather, a new suit, or a recent harrowing travel experience may be shared and, in fact, may often be brought up by the opponent. This should be encouraged. The parties are merely working toward a common ground and anything that will assist is good.

To illustrate, assume you have been diligently working at your present job for about a year, and you think it's high time that you received a raise. No one has mentioned it, so you decide to take the offensive and ask. As we've already learned, *you* should attempt to select the time that's most suitable to you. In addition, the place should be *your* work area instead of that of your boss, if that is at all possible. This is where many people seeking raises make one of their greatest mistakes. They pop the question or demand on their opponent's home field, namely, their boss' office. Naturally, the mere fact that they are seeking a raise will cause them some anxiety. Why, then, add to it by sinking into the chair in front of the boss' penetrating glare? So if you can't arrange to catch your boss in your work environment, at least attempt to do it on neutral ground—maybe after a meeting, in the shop, lunch room, or any other suitable, neutral place.

Now you want to begin the discussion in a friendly, positive vein, particularly if you anticipate any real resistance. Here's how an opening dialogue might look. Notice carefully how you bring your boss into a positive attitude in order to start off on the right foot.

Negotiator: "Good morning, Mr. Thomson. It's (the weather) a pleasant day."

Opponent: "Yes, it is, isn't it?"

Negotiator: "Makes one appreciate spring, doesn't it?"

Opponent: "Certainly does."

Negotiator: "I've taken care of the assembly problem. The results are on your desk."

Opponent: "Good. It's nice to have that one out of the way."

(Now you have him in the proper frame of mind. You can easily advance into the next phase by pointing out your excellent past service record with the company and then capping that off by asking for your raise.)

# 19

# Offensive Negotiation

"The way to prevent the enemy from attacking you is to attack him and keep right on attacking him. This prevents him from getting set." Those are the words of General George S. Patton, one of the most successful combat generals in the history of modern warfare.

Negotiation is very much like combat in that the negotiator is on the "front line" of the battlefield. It's therefore important for him to develop what he considers the best possible plan of action. The one that I most highly recommend and which brings the most favorable results is that of offensive negotiation.

## What Is Offensive Negotiation?

A young man recently asked me if I favored offensive negotiation. I said, "Yes." I noticed that the next several times we had the occasion to chat he came on so strong that I could hardly get a word in edgewise. It was clear that he didn't fully comprehend the meaning of offensive negotiation.

By offensive negotiation I refer primarily to a situation where the negotiator has gained the momentum and is thus preventing his opponenet from getting set. Often, when the opponent is on the run, he may be forced to make a concession that ordinarily would not have been made. And often, when the negotiator has decisively disproved an opponent's statement, it might make him much more reluctant to venture out with other similar statements for fear that they, too, may be successfully assailed. But offensive negotiation doesn't mean to overpower by uninterrupted talking, loud words, or pounding the table top with clenched fist. In most instances that would probably only make an opponent angry. Often only a few well-chosen words may do the trick, or even one timely question. When Ethan Allen, the Revolutionary War hero, was courting his favorite young lady, he frequently cut across a local cemetery. The people soon tired of his disregard for their dead and decided to cure him of the habit. One dark night he leaped the cemetery fence only to land at the bottom of a freshly dug grave. A figure in a white sheet immediately appeared above and uttered in a ghostly voice, "Ethan Allen, what art thou doing in my grave?" Unperturbed, Allen replied, "Well, what in thunder art thou doing out of it?" Notice how quickly the momentum changed. Allen's opponent (the ghostly figure) is probably still trying to come back after that one.

### When and How to Gain the Offensive

The negotiator should endeavor to take the offensive very early—the earlier the better. Also, it's important for him to learn to properly time himself. This means that he should take the offensive whenever he feels that he can do so without his opponent being consciously aware of the change. (If he is, the opponent will obviously immediately attempt to regain the lost momentum.) This, of course, can come only with a great deal of study and practice, as I will point out in the section on timing.

Ethan Allen's experience was one method of quickly and effectively gaining the offensive. Let's look at several more. One of General Patton's favorite techniques was to attack the enemy at its weakest points and to advance to the deepest possible point of penetration, regardless of his (Patton's) flanks. This would force the enemy to withdraw support from its stronger points in order to bolster the assailed weaker ones, thereby weakening the stronger points so that they, in turn, became vulnerable to attack. That's an excellent offensive negotiation technique. By concentrating on an opponent's weaker points you force him to devote more time and attention to them, both in the form of preparation and presentation. As he scurries to plug the holes of the points that are being directly assailed, his strong points suffer, since he must deprive them of the attention that they require. They become weaker and in turn may be similarly attacked.

To illustrate how this might be done, assume that there are four issues to be negotiated. One is definitely in the opponent's favor. Another could go either way—that is, each party's position is so close that neither can be said to dominate. The third is somewhat more favorable to the negotiator, and the fourth clearly in his favor. In such a situation it would normally be wisest for the negotiator to attempt to begin the negotiation by concentrating on his strongest issues; in other words, his opponent's weakest. The reader should recognize, of course, that in any negotiation it may sometimes not be possible to follow a precise order of issues. Discussions may frequently dictate the order. Nevertheless, in most, a negotiator should be able to guide or select the order. By this method he has initially taken the offensive. He thus has the momentum. His opponent was forced to concede.

What's the next step? The best would generally be to probe into the issue that may go either way or, if he feels that his momentum is strong enough at this point, to take up the issue that is most strongly in favor of his opponent. This will greatly enhance his chances of a favorable agreement on either of these two issues, since the opponent may have been forced to withdraw support from them and thus materially weakened them. If he meets with resistance, the negotiator can back off and move to the next most favorable issue to him. A successful agreement on that issue will provide him with additional momentum and thus afford him greater strength on the final two. It's almost always better to ride into issues that are either in favor of an opponent or, at best, equal, on the back of solid, positive momentum. Contrast that with initially attempting to win on these issues without any momentum, and you will see the tremendous advantage that offensive negotiation may afford.

Another good method to gain the offense is by concentrating on the language of an opponent. Frequently he will use broad, general terms to attempt to substantiate his position. If he does that, he's leading with his chin and, in effect, asking to be "knocked out" on that particular issue. This particular offensive technique can be employed in virtually every negotiation situation, large or small, and an opponent's utterances need not even be orally made.

To illustrate, assume you purchased a new swing set for the

kids. The sales literature states that the set is "strong, durable, and long-lasting." You try it, and in a week it starts falling apart. The seller is a discount house and not particularly interested in taking it back. In fact, its publicly advertised policy is that no refunds will be granted for returned goods once they've left the premises. They'll hit you with that policy the moment you walk in the door. You're thus immediately on the defensive and it will probably be difficult to get your money back or to get a replacement if you so desire. So to greatly enhance your chances, be prepared to *immediately* take the offensive and use their own sales literature to do it!

"I purchased this *strong, durable, long-lasting* swing set and it didn't last a week. What do you mean by strong? Durable? Long-lasting, etc., etc.?" Notice you didn't immediately ask for a refund. If you would have, the seller would have quickly fallen back on the publicly announced no refund policy, and thus switched the momentum. Certainly a refund (or a replacement) is your ultimate objective. But by concentrating on offensive tactics through use of your opponent's language, you can eventually get to that point by such means as suggesting that an "exception" be made in this case. The important point to remember, however, is that you've taken the offensive by use of your opponent's own language.

### What to Do Once the Offensive Has Been Gained

Once you have the offensive it is seldom wise to pause, or to play a defensive or conservative hand. The defense rarely scores points. Even when a defensive player recovers a fumble and runs for a touchdown, he has turned his thoughts to offensive tactics the moment he grabbed the ball and glanced down the field toward his opponent's goal. Defensive or conservation tactics after the offense has been taken may provide the opposition with just the opportunity he needs to turn the momentum around and win the game. It's much more difficult to regain the offense once it's been lost than to gain it at the outset. Counterattacks can be very costly in terms of preparation and presentation time, and results are often very dubious. It's almost always better to act than to react. Mere reaction rather than positive action when the walls are being stormed may soon lead to loss of the castle.

# 20

# Why It's Important to Determine Who Has Final Negotiating Authority

A frequent occurrence in negotiation is the presence of more than one person on the other negotiating side. I have participated in numerous such situations, with sometimes as many as six or more on the other side. This may present a real problem to the negotiator, since it is important for him to know who on the other side has final negotiating authority. By final negotiating authority, I refer to the person who is charged with the responsibility of making all final decisions at the negotiation. It is that person the negotiator must reach in order to succeed. Otherwise, he will have to rely upon the other side's subordinates to convince the one with authority. Most subordinates are simply not in a position to undertake such an effort, and even if they were, there can never be any assurance that they will succeed. In addition, the negotiator's entire approach may be fragmented and he would be, in effect, entrusting to others his job of demonstrating the soundness of his positions.

Frequently, in negotiating situations where the other side has more than one person present, there is no announcement as to which person has the final negotiating authority. Everyone is merely introduced, sometimes by titles, and everybody seems to freely join in the discussion. In such circumstances, I never allow the discussion to proceed without first determining who's in charge. An example of what can occur in such a situation might serve to illustrate why.

Often a negotiator is called upon to assist in negotiations which are already under way but are not proceeding favorably. I recall vividly one in particular. Negotiations had been carried on over a very long period with what was thought to be a general partner of a large investment house. Failing to get any productive action, I was requested to assist. Upon investigation, I discovered that the so-called "general partner" was really only a limited partner, with no authority to make binding decisions. My client, therefore, had to rely upon the limited partner to demonstrate to the general partners the soundness of his position—a very slender thread to rely upon. An immediate request was made that a general partner with final decision-making authority enter into the discussion. My request was granted, and the matter thereafter proceeded smoothly.

### How to Determine Who Has Final Negotiating Authority

The simplest and perhaps the most effective way to determine who has final negotiating authority is to ask. Yet it is not uncommon for many negotiators to fail to do so and, in some instances, fail even to concern themselves with this material aspect of negotiation. As earlier indicated, a negotiator may fruitlessly expend considerable time and energy "talking to the wrong guy." If the right guy is not present, the negotiator should wait until he is—or, if he is never present during the early stages of the negotiation, the negotiator should disclose only enough of his position to whet the other side's appetite in order to encourage them to bring in the person with final negotiating authority.

Another approach is to carefully examine titles and other similar labels of recognition of each person present on the other side. This technique, however, can be very misleading and thus fraught with considerable risk. Many large banks and other corporate entities, for example, have large numbers of vice presidents, executive vice presidents, and other titled officers. Some have very real authority, while others carry a title only. It can thus become very difficult for the negotiator to make an accurate judgment based upon title alone. When in doubt, I therefore always proceed beyond mere titles and tactfully inquire.

An experience here might serve to fully illuminate the danger of relying solely upon titles. The experience will also illustrate a third method of determining who has final negotiating authority, namely, by skillfully probing.

I was engaged in a negotiation with two persons present for the other side. One clearly, by his title, appeared to have final negotiating authority. The other was represented to have come along to "listen" or "audit" the negotiating sessions. In the early course of the discussions I began to suspect that the negotiator with the title was failing to exercise his authority, even though I knew he possessed the right to do so. I therefore decided to probe more deeply into the matter before continuing with the substance of the discussions.

Learning that the so-called, "silent" negotiator would be absent from the city on another matter, I requested that a negotiating conference be held with the titled negotiator. At first he refused. Through my insistence, however, he finally agreed. At the session I immediately plunged into an issue which was fairly non-controversial and one that I felt should ordinarily be readily agreed to. The opposing negotiator, however, refused to make a final commitment on the matter. Fidgeting nervously in his chair, he suggested on numerous occasions that he be allowed to have time to think it over. His predicament grew steadily worse as I brushed aside any reservations that he attempted to raise. Finally, he threw up his hands and simply said he would have to talk the matter over with the absent "silent" negotiator. It thus became clear that the absent negotiator was the one really possessing final negotiating authority. I welcomed his return. By skillfully probing I was able to direct my thoughts toward the person who was really making the decisions.

## Strategy After It Has Been Determined Who Has Final Negotiating Authority

Once the negotiator knows who has final negotiating authority, directing the thrust of his presentation toward that person may be done directly with him or indirectly, as the following experience will show.

During the course of preparation for the negotiation of an important matter, I learned that there would be three negotiators for the other side. I knew which one possessed final authority. The two others were specialists who would probably inquire into numerous matters and thus carry the brunt of the discussion. The influence of both on their superior was unknown, but I did know that the latter's final judgment was usually decisive. I therefore decided to direct my entire presentation toward him *even though I knew I would probably be talking directly to both of the specialists during most, if not all, of the negotiation.* In other words, my attitude was, let the other two ask what they want, the substance of my remarks will be directed toward the one who will be making the decisions.

Every matter raised by the specialists was so handled. When one raised what he thought was a serious reservation, my response was designed to relieve the one with authority. As the discussion continued, the man in charge soon began to show a lack of interest in many of the matters raised by his two subordinates. In addition, he not only argued against some of their questions but at one point even reprimanded one for asking what he thought to be an unnecessary question. Finally, he came completely over to my side.

## Joint Negotiating Authority

Occasionally in a negotiation the negotiator will encounter a situation where final authority rests jointly. Under such circumstances he can, of course, attempt to demonstrate the soundness of his position to all who possess the joint authority. This can make his task much more difficult, since the more persons that are involved in a final decision-making process, the less likelihood of getting a final decision.

Rather, the recommended course in those instances where the negotiator knows joint authority exists is to determine very early in the negotiation which of those possessing the joint authority is the stronger. The negotiator can thus direct the main portion, if not all of the substance of the discussion, toward that person, as I had done in my earlier example. If the negotiator can demonstrate to the stronger person the soundness of his position, he can to a great extent rely upon that person to, in effect, become his virtual ally in swaying the others.

To illustrate, I was involved in a negotiation of importance where I knew that the other two negotiators shared joint responsibility. One was a trial attorney charged with litigating the case in the event of nonagreement. The other, although possessing joint authority, could free himself completely from any subsequent responsibility should no agreement be reached and judgment by trial become necessary. After several conferences, neither appeared to be the stronger. Nevertheless, the one possessing the responsibility of trying the case was clearly much more exposed in the event of no settlement and would, I thought, therefore develop to be the stronger of the two. My assessment was reinforced by the fact that I was of the opinion that if litigation became necessary my client's chances of success were very strong. I, therefore, determined that the negotiations would be directed toward the trial aspects, with the hopes that the opposing negotiator assigned the responsibility of litigating the matter might be much more apt to see the merits of our position and to influence his colleague to do the same. It was successful.

# 21
# *Your Opponent*

The first and most important rule is to never judge your opponent by his appearance. As I've already indicated, a person's appearance will have a bearing upon his effectiveness. Nevertheless, it represents only his form or shell, the substance being his mental capability. Opponents come in all sizes and shapes. No two are ever alike, and their facial features and dress also generally cover the waterfront. The safest rule to follow, therefore, is to assume that your opponent will be equally as capable as you. If you prepare and negotiate on that basis, the dangers that are present from underestimating him can be largely avoided. This rule should be observed even though you may know your opponent well. Otherwise, you may consciously or subconsciously gauge the extent of your preparations on the basis of your opinion of him, and thus actually put yourself on his level of competence rather than far above where you belong. In addition, sometimes a younger opponent may have covered a lot of ground since the last time you negotiated with him and thus may have become a much more capable individual than you may think.

I've been up against some shrewd opponents who, if judged solely by their appearance, would probably not even merit an honorable mention. One in particular occurred some years ago. He appeared to be in his sixties, and looked so frail it seemed he would have difficulty mustering up enough strength to answer the opening bell. When it sounded, however, it didn't take him long to unleash the tiger that was hidden within him, and what followed was a very crisp and lively discussion of the issues.

A second important rule is to always try to discover as early in the negotiation as possible your opponent's motives for the positions that he takes or advances. Motives are what prompt people to act, and if you can discover what they are you'll also be able to predict the acts that will follow them. Why is he refusing to budge on a point or issue? What's the reason for him remaining silent on a particular matter? Why did he lead with a certain approach? The answers to these and many, many more are all designed to discover motives. Often these decisions must be made instantaneously, in the midst of discussions. This is another good example of where thorough preparation and knowledge of people pays off. As the discussions progress, learn to ask yourself these questions until they become second nature. Soon your ability to discover motives will increase, and you'll begin to sense the added efficiency that goes with it.

## Some Thoughts on the Types of Opponents You'll Encounter

Here are thumbnail sketches of the three basic types of individuals that you'll come upon. There are variations, of course, but most fall into these categories. Learn to discover which you're up against as early as possible in order to assist in developing your strategy, and also to avoid certain pitfalls that are inherent in dealing with each.

### THE STRONG TYPE

This type is very daring and unafraid. He likes to control things and frequently interrupts, often anticipating and answering questions before they're fully asked. He may forgive but seldom forgets. He makes decisions quickly and confidently, even if they later turn out to be in error. This is one of the quickest ways to spot him. There are very few gray areas in his way of thinking; everything is generally either black or white. He seldom errs because he prepares well. He's able to analyze well, but his haste in making decisions often offsets this. His appearance is generally very neat and precise; this is another good way to spot him. He takes pride in it and carries himself as if he wants others to know. He angers quickly and may even become angry when a position that *he* feels is reasonable is not accepted. On other occasions, he tends to feel sorry for himself for the same reason. This is why it's very important to explain in detail the reason or reasons any of his positions are not acceptable, and to always treat them seriously even though they may appear unrealistic. This type of individual is very easy to lead, particularly if your positions appear either black or white, and he's very responsive to reasonable suggestions or to positions that have been amply substantiated by facts, law or other means.

### THE VACILLATING TYPE

This type is very similar to the strong type, but differs in the following important respects.

He's generally not as dynamic and prefers to think things over. He seldom interrupts. He angers quickly but forgets just as quickly. He likes to consult outsiders or experts and likes to refer to them during discussion. This makes it harder to close. It's important, therefore, for your positions to be well substantiated in order to get him to make decisions. This type is just as capable as the strong type but generally doesn't prepare as well. He's more casual in his appearance and thus more prone to bad habits, such as allowing the tie to hang loosely around an unbuttoned collar. Clothes to him are secondary. (I once negotiated with one with a large hole in the heel of his sock.) He analyzes well. The quickest way to spot him is by the way he tends to put off decisions sometimes on even some of the smaller issues, and frequently asks for more supporting data or facts. This assists in making up for his lack of preparation and also provides him with more time to think.

### THE WEAK TYPE

This unfortunate fellow is very reluctant to make any decisions and would much rather have a higher-up to submit the data to and to make the decisions. Hence, he'll frequently ask to think things over. His uncertainty often makes him very nervous and subject to numerous bad habits, such as fingernail biting and squinting. Both his procrastination and bad habits are good clues to his identity. His dress runs all over the lot because his uncertainty allows him little if any time to concentrate on it. In most instances, it's better to bypass him and go to his higher-up rather than attempt to demonstrate to him and have him convince his superior. In fact, often the superior controls him to such an extent that he'll ask for information during the discussion without being able to justify the reason why. That's another good way to spot him. Be very patient with him and encourage him, and he'll respond as fully as he's able to.

In concluding this section I'd like to leave you with what I consider to be the Golden Rule of negotiation: *Treat your opponent as you would want him to treat you.* It doesn't mean that you shouldn't be tough and hard-hitting. On the contrary, it merely means that you should recognize him as a human being and treat him accordingly. You'll be the ultimate beneficiary!

# 22

# *Appealing to the Self*

*"Neither threats nor pleading can move a man unless
they touch some one of his potential or actual selves."*
William James

What's the best way for a man to motivate his wife? Appeal
to her self! If she enjoys baking bread and really throws herself
into the project, for example, he may marvel at her skills when
biting into a delicious slice that's covered with honey, or he may
comment on how cute she looks "with flour on her nose." In both
cases he's touched her self and she'll respond favorably. Similarly,
sincerely commenting on the beauty of the flowers that she so
expertly grows and arranges will please and motivate her. The
flowers are a part of her. And even telling her that she's got a
"green thumb" will please her. They all touch her as a housewife.
Touching her as a woman may mean a compliment on the beauty
of her eyes or hair. There she sees herself in an entirely different
role from that of a housewife. There she's a woman, and associates
different things with herself in that role.

It's important for the negotiator to understand that in order
to motivate his opponent, it's necessary that he adopt strategies
and techniques that appeal to his opponent's self. Notice that
James uses the term "selves." There is, according to many
psychologists, more than one self. One is concerned with the
objective elements of our life, such as our body, clothes, home,
relatives, friends, organizations that we belong to, and any other
matters that we connect with and consider a part of us. This is

generally referred to as "me." The other is the subjective or that
which is the thinking part of us. It's normally referred to as the
"I." Here, however, we'll use the term self to mean everything that
a person associates with himself in addition to what he thinks. In
other words, both the "me" and "I" will equal our self. It will
greatly simplify matters and adequately serve our purposes.

The early part of the negotiation is the best time to begin
probing for matters that are important to an opponent's self.
Common experiences tend to connect persons with one another. If
they have been employed in the same or similar capacities, been
members of the same civic or charitable organization, are from the
same neighborhood or background, or even both take their coffee
with cream and sugar, a common bond will exist between them.
When the negotiator knows that he shares a familiar experience
with his opponent, he should not be reluctant to dwell upon or
relive it. By doing so he's appealing to his opponent's self, and as
long as he's sincere, the relationship between them will grow
closer and the bond between them stronger.

Compliments appeal to the self. We've already touched upon
it with the housewife and woman. If an opponent is wearing an
exceptionally good-looking suit, a simple compliment, "That's a
very fine-looking suit you're wearing," will touch his self and
immediately warm him up. And if he says, "Thank you. My wife
happened to pick this one. She thinks I look good in brown," he's
provided the negotiator with another good opportunity to appeal
to his self. "She certainly has good taste," may be the reply. These
thoughts may appear simple, but both fully recognize the importance to the opponent of the clothes he's wearing and his spouse,
both intregal parts of his self. Sincerity, of course, is a must.
Sometimes you'll negotiate with an opponent with very striking
physical features, such as a strong physique or a thick, rich-looking
head of hair. In most instances you can bet that he's not only fully
aware of them (particularly if he's an older person), but also places
them high on the pedestal as a part of his self. The same would be
true of any of his intellectual accomplishments. If he is known for
his writings or ideas, for example, compliment him on them and
he'll respond.

Note from what I've already related that the technique of
appealing to an opponent's self has a two-fold objective. First, the

creation of a more compatible relationship with him as an individual. Never lose sight of the fact that negotiation, by its very definition, is a conferring between individuals. It's important, therefore, for the negotiator to fully realize that it's individuals he must influence in order to succeed. And to do so he must, as James proclaimed, reach "one of his potential or actual selves."

Second, by creating a more compatible relationship, he will actually be making himself a part of his opponent's self. This can easily be the case, for example, if there exists a strong enough connection between the two, such as coming from a common background or belonging to the same organizations. This latter objective makes it much easier to see the importance of appealing to the opponent's self. If the negotiator is a part of that self, even if only a small part, his words and the positions that he advances will be that much more beneficially received.

Just as favorably touching a person's self will positively motivate him, anything adversely affecting his self, whether intentional or unintentional, will offend him. Let me share a personal experience just to illustrate how easily and inadvertently one can hurt another's self.

I was watching a football game. The team made a bad blunder, and I said, "I'll bet the coach is pulling his hair out on that one!" Suddenly, I realized that the man sitting next to me possessed a physical feature common to many men, most of whom wish they never had it—baldness. The atmosphere suddenly became very cool. Fortunately, he was a stranger and the act was unintentional. Time thus quickly healed the hurt when the team suddenly caught fire. If I would have been negotiating and taken a similar approach, it could have cost me dearly. The moral? Be alert! Everything that comes from your opponent's actions and words will be telling you something about his self. If, during the preliminary discussions while exchanging pleasantries, he remarks that he took the family for a two week camping trip in the wilds and they "had the time of their lives," any adverse comments on his, yours or any other's outdoor experiences will have a repugnant effect. If you dislike the outdoors because of the bugs and mosquitoes, it's better to confine your remarks to the effect that you're pleased that he and his family enjoyed it. On the other hand, if you share his enthusiasm for the wilds, he's provided you with a perfect opportunity to appeal to his self. Again, sincerity is an absolute necessity.

Never be critical of matters that are irrelevant to the negotiation. If your opponent's flight was late, for example, never chastise either the airline or the pilot. Let him do it if he wants to. He may have a close relative or friend who works with an airline, or maybe even a brother who's a pilot.

Finally, it's important for the negotiator to realize that during the course of most negotiations many offenses will be committed against his self. Most will be unintentional, particularly if the opponent is unaware of the importance of appealing to another's self. Learn to disregard them. Remain entirely objective. Allowing your emotions to dominate is one of the quickest and surest ways of stifling negotiation progress.

# 23

# *The Place of Anger in Negotiation*

In order to fully appreciate the place of anger in negotiation it is essential that the negotiator understand certain basic ground rules. Knowledge of them will enable him to keep anger in its proper negotiating perspective rather than have it act as a teetering anchor, ready to drop at the first sign of danger and pull him down into a deep sea of uncertainty. Moreover, it will provide him with answers to such timely and important questions as: Should the negotiator ever lose his temper? Can anger ever be useful to the negotiator?

Before getting into the important elements of anger, it should be emphasized that no attempt is made here to discuss its numerous psychological aspects. That could easily take up volumes and would serve no useful negotiating purpose. Similarly, we are all generally aware of the physical reactions of an angry person. Shouting, harsh words, and even fist pounding, to name only a few, are not unusual.

## The Basics of Anger

When a person becomes angry, he experiences mental pain. Anger is thus a negative emotion. It's important to bear this in mind because whenever a person is under the influence of a negative emotion, it is generally not possible for him to either think or act constructively. Indeed, protracted negative emotions may be very harmful. Great remorse brought about by the death of a loved one or some other tragic event may lead to illness or even death if left unchecked. If pain, however, were the only feeling that a person experienced when he became angry, we could stop here and be guided by the simple but rigid rule that there is never any place for anger in negotiation. Unfortunately, this is not the case.

The most basic reason a person becomes angry in the first place is because he *feels* that he has been wronged—that a personal slight has been committed against either him or someone or something close to him. If he feels that someone has called him a name, for example, he will generally become angry. Likewise, if he feels someone has injured his property or perhaps a loved one without justification, he will become angry. Attacking one of his principles will make him angry.

Note that I have placed emphasis on the word "feel." Whether in fact the angered person has been wronged is immaterial. So long as he feels that he has, he will experience anger. His pain, however, will soon be replaced by a feeling of confidence. It's a sort of temporary confidence, fostered mainly by the desire for revenge. This, as we will see, is where anger becomes directly relevant to negotiation.

## Anger's Influence Upon Negotiation

Bolstered by this feeling of confidence excited mainly by the desire for revenge, the angry negotiator may say or do things which can be highly detrimental to his position. In addition, his temporary confidence can make him feel as if he is completely justified in any position he takes and he thus may be unwilling to even discuss any alterations, no matter how reasonable they may be.

To illustrate, I had the occasion very early in my professional career to negotiate a matter with two old and very experienced attorneys. I knew from the moment I laid eyes upon them that they would be difficult. One had heavy, bushy eyebrows and a bulldog-like jaw that had undoubtedly chewed up many opponents. The other, the taller of the two, was very smooth and meticulous in both manner and speech. Both pretty much had their way until one became angry and lost sight of his negotiating base. Oddly enough, it was the polished one. Anger thus became my ally—his enemy!

When negotiations have reached an apparent standstill, anger may sometimes step in to provide an opening for resumption. I am not suggesting here that the negotiator deliberately set out to make his opponent angry. But what I do want to point out is that often, when the parties are at a standstill, an opponent may be highly prone to become angry. By being alert, the negotiator may seize upon his opponent's anger as an opportunity to get the matter back to the bargaining state. This may often be a fairly easy thing to do. The opponent's anger-created confidence generally makes him boldly state his position, which actually serves as the lead-in for the negotiator to resume the discussions. It happens quite often, and if the negotiator's explanation is tactful enough, he should, in most instances, be able to not only cool his opponent's temper down, but also push on toward a successful conclusion.

To relate it to an everyday occurrence, assume that you have been feuding with your neighbor because her young Saint Bernard is constantly trampling through your flower bed. You've repeatedly called it to her attention and now, tired of being reminded, she becomes angry and says: "Quit bothering me about my dog. I can't control him. And besides, he can go where he pleases. It's still a free country!"

"Do you really feel he can?" you ask in a somewhat resigned tone (remaining completely cool, of course. What you're doing is pointing out the unreasonableness of her position).

" . . . Yes! . . . " She replies, still firm but waivering. (You've caught her somewhat off guard.)

"I guess maybe I shouldn't really be planting any more flowers, then. But I hate to give it up. They're so pretty," you reply, still somewhat resigned. (You're emphasizing the unreasonableness of her position even more.)

"Well . . . They are, aren't they. Maybe I can get the dog trained. He's still very young." (Her anger has subsided. She's gotten the message.)

"I'm sure you can. And after he is, I'd like to have him over. The kids like him very much."

This brings up another important aspect of anger. It is always related to the self. That is, the act that prompted it must have been directed toward the individual. If he is a member of a certain group, he may or may not become angry for an offense directed against the group depending, upon how closely associated he feels he is to the group. If a person declares, for example, that all real estate men are not to be trusted and he is then dealing with a real estate man, the chances are good that the real estate man will feel slighted, particularly if he has been a long standing member of the group or makes his livelihood from selling. Likewise, a statement to the effect that all bankers are rich and prey upon the poor will not fare too well when attempting to get a loan for that new car or braces for the kid's teeth. Offhand remarks such as these serve no useful purpose in negotiation and should be avoided.

Deal objectively and leave remarks that are likely to make your opponent angry out of the negotiation! Otherwise, run the risk of anger—the resulting confidence—and the consequences that follow it.

## What to Do When Your Opponent Has Become Angry

The important thing to remember here is that anger is only temporary. The passage of time, therefore, may often dull or eliminate it entirely. There is thus much wisdom to Thomas Jefferson's rule: "When angry, count ten before you speak; if very angry, a hundred."

A showing that there is no justification for the anger (the Saint Bernard case) or perhaps a gesture of equal or greater degree than the act that caused the anger may also subside it. A simple apology is. an example of an equal or greater gesture if the act which caused the anger is not too severe. If severe, something more is generally necessary, such as some form of explanation, concession, or other offering.

## Should a Negotiator Ever Become Angry?

From what I have already written, it seems clear that displays of anger on the negotiator's part should be avoided. They cannot materially assist and may, in fact, prove very harmful. Coolness and objectivity should be the order of the day. Like most other useful qualities, they can come only with experience and the development of a strong will.

The only real exception is what I like to refer to as "controlled" anger. The opportunity for its use generally comes about when the negotiator has cause to become angry because of some slight directed against either him or his client. For example, I was asked to aid in a negotiation that had drawn out over a long period of time. I suspected that the other side was deliberately using dilatory tactics, a technique which I have always deplored. When my suspicions became confirmed, I displayed anger. My emotions, however, remained completely under control. Only my voice disclosed displeasure. My opponent's dilatory tactics provided me with complete justification. There was little danger, therefore, in making him angry *so long as I did not broaden the sphere of my justification.* In other words, my remarks had to be confined to his use of delaying tactics and our intended course, should serious negotiation not immediately commence. I could thus take full advantage of the slight and turn it around into a negotiating aid. If I would have gone too far, however, and provided him with justification for becoming angry, the shoe would have quickly shifted to the other foot—my opponent's. Use of controlled anger is therefore very risky, and when to use it and how far to go must be governed largely by experience and each individual situation. If a person is required to do extensive negotiation, however, I highly recommend that he learn to master its application.

# 24

# *The Necessity for Equalization*

Equalization is a vital part of any negotiation—so important, in fact, that a negotiator can never expect to be consistently successful until he has fully recognized and mastered it.

I have witnessed numerous negotiations where one side will advance certain arguments in support of his position, and his opponent will never really bother to consider them. Sometimes he'll simply disregard them. On other occasions he'll treat them very passively in an attempt to shrug them off, hoping that they'll somehow go away or his opponent will forget them. It's sort of like a man living in a penthouse atop a tall building who, upon hearing that a fire is about to gut both the elevators and staircase on the lower floor, simply says to himself, "Who cares? There are forty fireproof floors separating me from the flames." Wait until it comes time for him to walk the family poodle!

## What Is Equalization?

Perhaps the best way to define equalization is to picture a scale of the beam balance variety, a sensitive little instrument frequently used in laboratories. Negotiation, like a beam balance, is often very delicate. In virtually every negotiation the negotiator's opponent will advance certain arguments which support his position. As Figure 1 demonstrates, if these arguments are left to stand, the weight of them may tip the precariously balanced beam in the opponent's favor and make it highly improbable for

107

the negotiator to attain a favorable agreement. Since his opponent's arguments are the only cards placed on the table, the stakes,
at this point at least, belong to him.

If, on the other hand, the negotiator is able to refute,
distinguish or neutralize his opponent's arguments, his chances of
reaching a favorable agreement will be greatly enhanced. As Figure
2 illustrates, he's placed equal weights on the scale and the beam is
perfectly balanced. This is a state of complete equalization. Even
if the negotiator never advances one positive argument on his own
behalf, he still would stand a chance of reaching a favorable
agreement, all other things being equal. It's essential for the
negotiator to realize that he *must reach at least this point in every
negotiation* in order to be consistently successful.

The ideal position is represented in Figure 3. Here the
negotiator has not only wisely equalized his opponent's arguments, but has advanced arguments of his own which have not
been equalized by his opponent. The delicately balanced beam has
thus tipped in his favor. He has attained and gone beyond the state
of equalization—three aces to one, if you will. All other things
being equal, a favorable agreement should be reached.

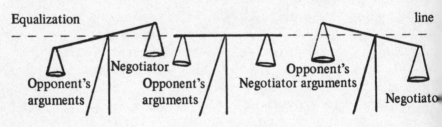

Figure 1. Negotiator
has failed to equal-
ize opponent's argu-
ments.

Figure 2. Negotiator
has completely equal-
ized opponent's argu-
ments.

Figure 3. Negotiator
has equalized opponent's
arguments and advanced
his own, which have not
been equalized.

## How to Attain Equalization

There are a variety of ways to attain equalization. A good
one is for the negotiator to simply refute his opponent's
arguments by demonstrating that they are not well founded. Fo

example, assume that a person is attempting to negotiate the sale of a home by alleging, among other things, that the property taxes are low and should remain fairly stable over the ensuing years. This may be easily disproved simply by producing evidence of past tax increases together with the steadily increasing costs of local governments, which derive a large share of their tax dollars from property taxes. Or perhaps an opponent is arguing that gross rentals of an office building have been projected out to a certain figure, even though they are now much lower. This can be refuted, for example, if it can be shown that the vacancy rate of the property has consistently run much higher than comparable properties due to such factors as physical deterioration and poor location.

Another good method is to distinguish the opponent's arguments. To illustrate, if the subject of discussion is a shopping center lease and the landlord wants a percentage of the gross sales in addition to a fixed rental, which he argues is fairly standard in shopping center leases, it might be pointed out that anticipated sales will be relatively higher than other tenants in the center and it would be inequitable to penalize a potentially successful tenant when a fixed rental should amply compensate the landlord for the space. Or, if a real estate salesman or business broker is attempting to justify the sales price of a home or business by using sales of other homes or businesses, distinguishing why these homes or businesses are not comparable should be the equalizer. Perhaps the homes are not even located in the same neighborhood, or the businesses may produce dissimilar products or are capitalized differently. On the other hand, if the salesman or broker firmly believes that the sales are in fact comparable and facts have not been brought to his attention to distinguish them, it may prove very difficult to get him to lower his price unless, of course, other equalizing factors are introduced.

This brings us to another good approach to attain equalization, namely, by advancing arguments which are of equal or greater weight. This method has an additional advantage because it is entirely an offensive tactic. It recognizes the validity of the opponent's arguments but says, in effect, mine are of equal or greater weight. The beam is thus again balanced and there is a state of equalization, or perhaps even one where the scale is tipped in the negotiator's favor. In the last illustration above, producing other comparable home or business sales to offset or equalize the opponent's would be a good example.

Finally, demonstrating to the opponent that his arguments are not relevant or material to even warrant a place on the scale is still another good method to attain equalization. To illustrate here, I'll draw from an experience. Lawyers are frequently called upon to examine court opinions of all varieties. During the course of a negotiation, my opponent attempted to argue that a then recent court opinion had a material bearing upon the matter being negotiated. When it was pointed out that the decision was not applicable to past transactions and therefore irrelevant, the argument was completely dropped.

## Conclusion

In concluding this section, I want to again emphasize the importance of the need for equalization. Don't be like the man in the penthouse, completely oblivious to arguments that will directly affect him. Equalize your opponent's arguments as early and as effectively as possible. It's essential to consistent negotiation success!

# 25

# *Avoiding the Danger of Inversion*

The order of importance of issues is generally governed by either the amount of dollars involved or the impact upon people, or both. An issue involving one million dollars should obviously command more effort and concentration than one involving only one thousand dollars. Similarly, an issue involving the job security of hundreds of employees or the profitability of a company should command more respect and attention than one of lesser importance. Unfortunately, this is often not the case.

As you've probably already guessed, inversion as I am using the term in this discussion simply means spending more time on smaller issues to the detriment of larger ones. At first glance, this may seem like a very elementary proposition. After all, everyone knows the difference and has enough horse sense to concentrate on the larger. But smaller issues are generally less complex and thus easier to understand than larger ones. In addition, there is usually less pressure associated with them, since people are often not accustomed to dealing with larger issues. These factors lead one toward a natural tendency to not only feel more comfortable with smaller issues, but to consciously and unconsciously dwell upon them. The danger of inversion is thus present in virtually every negotiation, and negotiators frequently fall into its unsuspecting trap.

Often inversion can creep into the discussion so subtly that the negotiator may not realize what's happening until it's too late. To illustrate, during the course of a large and complicated

111

negotiation, one of the issues concerned the price of a corporation's common stock. Discussions were held on a per share basis and we were initially only about fifteen dollars per share apart on a final price. Standing alone, this was relatively a small amount and it would appear to have been easy to resolve the matter. But there was in excess of one hundred thousand shares involved. The ultimate difference was thus in excess of one and one-half million dollars! The same applies to acreages or other assets that run into large numbers. Fifty dollars per acre may not seem like much, but if hundreds or even thousands of acres are involved, it can quickly add up to a very tidy sum. So if your opponent (often intentionally) attempts to negotiate on a per share or per acre basis, never lose sight of the overall impact of what's being advanced. Carry the multiples through mentally as the discussion progresses or stop to compute the figure, if necessary. He may be attempting to disguise a larger issue, hoping that during the heat of battle inversion will draw you into its tenacious grasp and thus work to your detriment.

Winning on smaller issues can be an important means of building up positive momentum and conditioning an opponent toward your way of thinking on the larger issues, but winning battles and losing wars is not the surest road to survival. Hence, all other things being equal, it's far better to sacrifice smaller issues to win the larger ones. So concentrate on the big ones and always maintain a keen vigil for that unsuspecting but often very damaging culprit called *Inversion!*

# 26

# *How Anxiety Can Affect a Negotiation*

One of my first experiences with anxiety as a negotiating aid came about when I was a young lawyer fresh out of law school. I was assigned the difficult and unrewarding task of collecting numerous small debts due to a large automobile dealership which was in the process of liquidation. Not desiring to become involved with many small and bothersome lawsuits or wanting to shower the debtors with letters and telephone calls, I decided to employ a new and different approach.

I carefully drafted a form letter. It consisted of two quite simple paragraphs. The first merely acknowledged the existance of the debt. The second related that if payment was not received by the date specified therein, "appropriate action" would be taken which would necessarily result in "additional expense" to the debtor over and above that already due. In other words, the letter simply left to the imagination of the debtor the numerous and varied possible consequences of his further neglecting to pay, with the clincher being the likelihood of a much greater cash outlay for failure to do so.

What happened? The majority of the debts were promptly paid prior to the deadline date. The possibility of additional action together with the danger of incurring increased expenses prompted a feeling of anxiety that operated as an effective lever to the benefit of all, including the debtors.

The foregoing experience is a relatively simple one. Nevertheless, it illustrates the effect anxiety may have upon an indiv-

113

idual and how it can motivate him toward positive action. It's important for the negotiator to understand this and to maintain his awareness of it during the course of any negotiation.

## How to Make Effective Use of Anxiety

There are numerous ways in which the negotiator can make effective use of anxiety. The best is for him to make his opponent aware of some imminent harm or danger which may have an important effect upon him. A mother adopts this method when she advises her child to "Clean up your room or no television tonight!" A policeman uses it when he warns a driver that he will be given a traffic ticket the next time he is caught speeding; the skilled attorney employs it when he advises the other party to a contract that his client will sue if complete performance is not immediatley undertaken.

All are everyday occurrences and represent the most basic use of anxiety. In each a picture of a harmful or adverse circumstance is painted. Anxiety then appeared and joined forces with the mother, policeman and lawyer. It can similarly ally itself with the negotiator who chooses to make his opponent aware of any adverse circumstances which may affect him or his client. A young teacher friend recently employed this technique to perfection. Wanting to assign her students a special research project but not having sufficient books available in the school library, she decided to check them out of the public library. The librarian, however, told her quite frankly that such a large number of books could not be checked out by only one person. She was not one to be discouraged easily, and after pondering the matter a moment, the teacher very sweetly inquired whether the librarian would mind if she brought one hundred and thirty twelve- and thirteen-year-old children to the library several nights a week for the next several weeks to do their research. The librarian literally gasped. The teacher got her books!

At this point I think it is well that the reader make note of one important fact. Anxiety is merely a state of mind, nothing more. A strong person who is able to not take counsel of his fears will ordinarily be able to thwart the effects of anxiety. The same holds true of a person who has forgotten the adverse circumstances which may have a harmful effect upon him. This is fairly common in negotiations which run over long periods of time. The negotiator should therefore be careful not to allow his opponent's forgetfulness to work against him, and should take every reasonable opportunity to keep any adverse matters fresh in his opponent's mind.

Another important manner in which the negotiator may count on anxiety as an aid is to be certain not to advance positions or opinions that are either unnecessary or unreasonable. This occurs quite often in negotiation, particularly when the negotiator is relatively inexperienced, and frequently leads to lack of a successful agreement on the matter being negotiated. If the negotiator, for example, unnecessarily confides that no other purchasers are interested in the property that he is attempting to negotiate for sale, he is insulating his opponent from knowledge of competition, a factor which can cause considerable anxiety. If he acknowledges that a similar attempt to sue on the grounds that he is now alleging met with failure and he is not optimistic about his own chances, he is eliminating any fear of loss to the other side. If he offers five hundred thousand dollars for a piece of property that he knows is worth four times that much, he is banishing any fear by the seller that he may pass up a good deal. The examples can go on and on. The foregoing, however, sufficiently illustrate the need for the negotiator to exercise good judgment in the positions and opinions that he advances.

The negotiator may also utilize the effects of anxiety by taking care not to make his opponent angry. Why? Because, as I related in a previous section, anger is always accompanied by a feeling of confidence, and a confident person cannot at the same time suffer from anxiety. The two are opposites. When confidence appears, anxiety departs. Thus, by making his opponent angry, the negotiator may be sacrificing anxiety as an important negotiating aid—a high price, indeed, for a slip of the tongue or some other act which can raise the dander of another. In any negotiation, but particularly those where the issues are large or of great public interest, emptions are apt to run very high and anger is always a clear and present danger. It may therefore become a real challenge for the negotiator to steer clear of this pitfall and to guide his opponent tactfully toward an open and objective viewpoint on the issues.

## How to Reduce or Eliminate Anxiety

Every negotiator must realize that as a human being he can be as much prone to the feeling of anxiety as his opponent. It therefore becomes important for him to adopt measures to protect himself from its gripping and harmful effects.

Perhaps the most effective method to substantially minimize or completely escape from any feeling of anxiety is for the negotiator to anticipate the basic weaknesses in his own negotiating position and to take steps to deal with them. An experience here might serve to better illustrate how this may be done.

During the preparation for the negotiation of a very large matter, I became aware of a glaring deficiency in my client's position due, primarily, the to existance of adverse court decisions. I knew that the matter was certain to be raised by the other side and I, therefore, set about to prepare for it prior to the bargaining sessions. My approach was simply this. Having thoroughly researched all of the existing law on the subject, I then spent several "long" hours drafting a response to the expected inquiry. My response consisted of one short, simple sentence with carefully chosen language. I rehearsed the sentence and the tone of voice that I wanted to say it in until both were firmly committed to memory and could be spoken with ease. This is one of the very few instances where I have actually resorted to the use of a rehearsed statement. In most cases I do not recommend it, because it generally leads to artificialness. During the latter part of the discussion, when the expected challenge finally came, I was, of course, fully prepared to answer it. Any feeling of anxiety on my part had left me long ago after I first discovered the deficiency. Thorough preparation had replaced it with a feeling of confidence, which was carried into the bargaining. My response was immediate. The impact was great enough to settle the matter.

Another method to reduce or eliminate the effects of anxiety is for the negotiator to either find an alternate to the adverse facts and circumstances which have caused it, or to instill even a greater feeling of anxiety in the other side. What the negotiator is saying here, in effect, is that if I can't prepare to meet it head on, I'll find a way around, over, or under it. If that won't work, I'll fight fire with a greater fire. A very wealthy business friend of mine used this latter approach very effectively when threatened with what he felt was an unwarranted lawsuit. "You sue me," he said, "and I'll defend myself with every penny I own!" Faced with an enormous potential out-of-pocket expense against such a well-stocked individual with only dubious results possible, the threatening party backed down.

Using the "finding an alternate approach" system can have similarly effective results. If the parties are close on the price of a parcel of real estate, for instance, and the opponent has remained firm on the sale price and also advised that others have expressed an interest in the property, the negotiator may indicate that the purchaser also has another piece of property in mind and will certainly proceed to consider it if the price is not reduced. Or, to relate it more to an everyday occurrence, if the plumber wants two hundred dollars for a small sewer cleaning job or he'll turn the account over to his lawyer for collection, the lady of the house might counter with, "Please do. I can't be out more than two hundred dollars anyway, and your legal fees will soon exceed that." If the strong-willed lady of the house wanted to carry it one step farther into the "greater feeling of anxiety" approach (if she felt the plumber was really out of line), she might continue with, "I'm sure a judge will welcome the opportunity to see just how you do your business!" Then simply sitting tight should get her a reduced bill equal in measure to the work performed. Not only did she eliminate her anxiety but she put the burden right on the back of her plumber friend.

# 27

# *Simplicity*

Simple ideas work best and receive the greatest following because they're the easiest to understand. The more complex a negotiator makes his presentation, the more difficult his task will become. Explanations piled upon explanations in order to get across a point may easily lead to confusion. It therefore behooves him to keep his approach very simple and basic. The simpler and more basic, the better.

I've already stressed in previous sections the importance of using simple language and the need for reducing preparation to as simple a task as possible. The negotiator's quest for simplicity, however, should not end there, but should necessarily spill over into every other aspect of the negotiation. For example, when confronted with a complex matter that may call for lengthy explanation or discussion, break it down into sections or individual components and explain each one separately, with perhaps a brief summary showing how they all fit together like pieces of a jigsaw puzzle. If your opponent still doesn't comprehend, don't fault him. Remember, the burden is always upon you to demonstrate the merits of your positions. Look for a better way to explain, perhaps breaking the matter down into even greater detail, but always keeping it simple. Learn to anticipate when and what type of simplicity is called for. This may vary from opponent to opponent.

Assume that you want to negotiate a lease with a man and wife who want to start a small family business. Neither has any prior business experience. He is a retired army officer and she is a housewife. You're an experienced real estate man representing the property owner. In your trade you're accustomed to dealing with experienced business renters, and ordinarily when the rental question comes up, it's discussed in terms of square feet and price per square feet. But why do that here? Why not keep it simple? Forget about square feet in this case. It will probably only generate uncertainty. It would be better to approach it on an annual or monthly basis: "This property will rent for $450 per month, or $5,400 per year." They can inspect it for proper size or you can give them your opinion when you learn the nature of their intended business. In many cases it may not even be necessary to mention square feet.

In the above situation, if the potential renter is experienced, perhaps even another real estate man negotiating for a client, square footage and cost per square foot would be the simplest approach.

Simplicity may mean hardly speaking at all. I once negotiated a matter where my opponent did virtually all of the talking in an attempt to convince me of the merits of his position. Why interrupt when unnecessary? Better to keep it simple.

Finally, never assume that because a negotiation is complex, with many issues and twists and turns, that it cannot be crystallized into simple components and discussed on that basis. On the contrary, negotiation success means simply effective communication, and the more I negotiate, the more I realize that by far the best way to attain it is through simplicity in everything that the negotiator does.

# 28

# *Timing*

Like everything else in life, timing is an essential part of any negotiation. There is, indeed, a time to make an offer and a time to reject one; a time to speak and a time to remain silent; and, yes, even a time to strategically postpone the negotiations.

To illustrate, if you have been waiting for some time to hear from your opponent and he finally telephones and suggests an immediate conference, perhaps even the next day, you can be certain that he's prepared to the hilt and raring to negotiate. The wisest course under such circumstances might be to set a date later, say in a week or ten days. This will throw him off stride, similar to a boxer who is all prepared and keyed up for the big fight only to have it postponed for a week. It makes him retrain to keep fit just as it will your opponent, and chances are that neither will ever reach the state of preparedness that existed prior to the postponement. It thus facilitates the negotiator's timing and throws off his opponent's.

It's very difficult to put down in writing not only the importance of good timing, but also how to develop it, simply because the situations where it's necessary in any negotiation can literally run into the hundreds. This, of course, includes good timing on all matters, both large and small. I will therefore limit my discussion to emphasizing its importance, together with several illustrations of a hypothetical nature in order to demonstrate its application.

As I have already indicated, virtually *everything* the negotiator does is dependent upon good timing. Compare it to a chess game. It often takes that much thought and finesse. Don't expect to checkmate the opponent's king with clumsy moves, like one under the influence of alcohol trying to walk a straight line. If your opponent has any skill at all, you'll need well-timed moves to even hope to win his king.

How can you develop a good sense of timing? The best way is by constant practice in order to accumulate the experience and personal judgment that is indispensable to good timing. This requires constant reflection by the negotiator. When he makes a well-timed proposal, for example, he usually can tell by the favorable reaction from his opponent. He should think about it. Know precisely why it turned out to be so good. Engrain it within his mind. He can thus consider whether similar timing may be applicable in other like situations. Perhaps good timing on many may only require a slight variation. He will be in a much better position to make this judgment if he knows why he was successful in the first case.

The same applies to matters that involve bad timing. It's inevitable that any negotiator, regardless of how skillful he is, will say or do something that is poorly timed. He should know why his timing was off. It's human to error in the first instance, even though it sometimes may be costly. But as the old saying goes, to stumble over the same stone twice is a proverbial disgrace. A successful negotiator simply cannot afford to make the same mistake twice.

What is the best time to convey to the opponent that his offer is being rejected? Is it at the commencement of the negotiation, assuming that the negotiator knows beforehand that it will probably be rejected, as is sometimes the case? Or maybe after the opponent has begun or even completed his presentation, even though the negotiator knew beforehand that the opponent's proposal would be rejected? Maybe the negotiator would like to use the opponent's demonstration as a basis for going into his own proposal. He might, in such a situation, want to allow his opponent to get well into his presentation, or maybe even finish it, before a rejection. It may make it much easier for the opponent to accept a rejection and listen to the negotiator's proposal. This technique can often be very successful, but only if properly timed. The opponent must feel that he has had an opportunity to say his fill. Ordinarily, it would be highly difficult for any opponent to sit there and listen to an alternate proposal if he hasn't even been afforded the opportunity to put forth his own. Personalities could conceivably become involved and no progress made. Why? All because of improper timing.

Take another example of how timing can have an important effect on the outcome of any negotiation. Assume the negotiator is about to make a proposal to a large corporation that is experiencing financial difficulties on how the corporation can increase its sagging sales and profits. The negotiator learns, either directly or indirectly, that another corporation is interested in purchasing the troubled corporation and is about to make an offer for it. Does the negotiator attempt to make his proposal prior to the commencement of any negotiations between the corporations? He could easily come to that conclusion, his thinking being that his idea will materially assist the sagging corporation and thus place it in a stronger bargaining position with the prospective purchaser, or perhaps even allow it to continue to go along on its own. On the other hand, postponing his proposal until the corporations are well into their negotiations may be equally as beneficial, since it may give a shot in the arm to the acquiring corporation's interest in the sagging corporation and thus enhance the chances of the negotiator's success.

The key is all in the timing. By timing his proposal right, the negotiator's task can become that much easier. Poor timing, on the other hand, may make it that much more difficult.

I cannot overemphasize the importance of good timing in everything that the negotiator does in any negotiation. He should strive to perfect it on every occasion. Good timing is like a well-swung bat meeting the ball at just the right instant. It's much more apt to send it flying out of the park for a home run and thus a score. Practice it at every opportunity!

# 29

# *The Importance of Observation*

*"If you don't use your eyes for seeing,
you will need them for weeping."*
Friedrich Foerster

One of the biggest mistakes the negotiator can make is to become a slave to the paper and pencil. As he becomes accustomed to the ways of others, he'll soon realize that the blink of an eye, wrinkle of the face, and even a twitch of the nose can have some significance. It may be providing him with valuable clues as to his opponent's motives, habits, the strategies and techniques he's employing, his sincerity, and even the extent of his organization.

For these reasons, note taking during the course of any negotiation should be limited to recording only what are considered to be essential points. These include such matters as the agreement reached and commitments made, such as agreeing to provide additional information by either the negotiator or his opponent, or others that the negotiator wants to be certain not to forget. Otherwise, the negotiator's attention should be fixed (if not glued) upon his opponent.

Facial features can be very revealing. Is your opponent smiling? Why? Is it because he recognizes the importance of a warm, friendly smile? Or perhaps he's pleased with himself. Why? How about that frown? Is it natural or intentional? Sometimes a person will fake a frown in order to make it appear as if he's displeased when inside he's elated. Unfortunately, you can't look into your opponent's mind to determine his motives. Knowledge of people, of course, will materially assist.

Another important aid is observation. If your opponent fails to look you in the eye when making an important proposal, it generally presents you with two possibilities. He may either have developed a very bad habit, in which case he'll repeat it throughout the discussions, or he may lack sincerity. Maybe he doesn't believe in the proposal he's making or is representing a strong-willed client who has taken an extreme position which is difficult for him to justify.

I recently negotiated a matter where my opponent slightly bowed his head as he was about to make an important proposal. That simple act telegraphed his lack of faith in what he was advocating. If I would have had my attention diverted elsewhere, perhaps needlessly taking notes or gazing out the window, I would have missed this significant outward indication of his sincerity.

Carefully observing your opponent will provide you with important insight on the thoroughness of his organization. If he fumbles around for important papers or carries large files that appear disorganized, with papers even sticking out of them as though they were hurriedly crammed into place, you can ordinarily assume that his attention will be diverted whenever he has to recall or search for an important document.

His appearance will tell you a great deal about him. Is he well groomed? I recently negotiated with an opponent who was overly neat and precise. His appearance not only unmistakably pointed toward the type of individual he was, but also the importance he placed upon recognition. It enabled me, of course, to adopt strategies and techniques to suit the situation.

## Lateral Vision

Whenever there is more than one opponent or the opponent's client is present, it is important for the negotiator to extend his observation to all of the parties present. His primary concentration, of course, should be centered on the one doing the talking. Second, however, is that he realize that the actions of everyone present may serve as a valuable aid. In an earlier section I pointed out how I was able to discover how several opponents had prearranged a system whereby the one outside of my direct view could signal the other as the negotiation progressed, and how one was taking the liberty to peer at any work papers that I set before myself. I was able to do this primarily through the use of lateral vision. When a person on the other side is present who is relatively unskilled in the art of negotiation, his intentions are often mirrored on his face as he reacts to the discussions.

The negotiator should learn to use his lateral vision to actually watch everyone present on the other side and to thus capitalize on these situations. Just as the skillful trial attorney will wisely employ his lateral vision in carefully observing the witnesses, jury, and opposing counsel, the keen negotiator will likewise fix his attention on all of his opponents.

# 30

# When to Take "No" for an Answer

"The answer is definitely no!"

That was the response I was confronted with at the first session on a matter that I wanted very badly to close. My position, I felt, was very reasonable. My opponent, however, had apparently decided to the contrary and had closed the door. Or had he?

I often chuckle at the story of the successful old country salesman who, when asked by his boss at what point he gave up on a potential customer, replied: "Depends which one of us kicks the bucket first." The cagey old man's reply probably goes to an extreme as far as negotiation is concerned. Nevertheless, it does illustrate the fact that persistence and success are frequent companions.

Remember that a "no" answer is more than just a word. It generally carries with it a person's considered judgment, backed by what he feels is experience. He is putting his "self" on the line. Accordingly, when confronted with a negative response, the negotiator must immediately set out to discover the available means to overcome it. Sometimes this may be done by making certain that his opponent is fully aware of all of the facts. Maybe a reiteration of the merits of his rejected proposal will do the trick, or he may alter his strategy and approach the discussion from a fresh avenue. Whatever the case, he must display persistence. By doing this, his opponent's resistence will often falter and his position can be traced to look something like this: "NO . . . No . . . no . . . ? . . . mayBE . . . YES." Remember that the important thing is for the other side to ultimately say "Yes." It seldom makes any difference whether the affirmative response comes early or late in the negotiation—so long as it comes!

A word of caution is due here. Under no circumstances should the negotiator ever place himself in the position of begging, pleading or haggling. Not only is such conduct degrading, but it can often lead to failure. Once the negotiator has resorted to such tactics, frequently no further fruitful exchange on the merits can be expected. His chances of success have thus diminished considerably and perhaps even fully escaped him. In addition, he may have damaged his rapport with his opponent for any possible future contacts on other matters.

Now let's return to the negative response that I was confronted with. Here is what subsequently happened. I asked my opponent to hold off on a final decision until I had a chance to dig up additional facts which might shed more light on the merits of my position. He agreed. On my second try he remained firm. On my third, he began to waiver. On the fourth session he weakened considerably. On the *fifth* he said "Yes." Moral? I think it's clear. *Never*—I repeat—*Never* give up until every reasonable means has been exhausted. I can think of nothing more essential to successful negotiation than persistence!

# 31

# *Principle vs. Personality*

Our purpose here is to discuss those numerous instances when principle or personality may become involved in a negotiation. In negotiation, both sides are (or should be) desirous of obtaining definite objectives. There is, therefore, always either a greater or lesser degree of opposition, depending upon the facts and circumstances of each particular case—and whenever there's opposition, it's bound to sometimes involve principle, often personality, and sometimes both.

Each negotiator must, of course, stand firmly upon principles that he believes and has faith in. Moreover, the safest rule for him to follow is to never involve personalities in the negotiation. But what about those situations where his opponent or the opponent's client has invoked either principle or personality, or both? What should the negotiator do in such circumstances? Remember, the ultimate objective in any negotiation is to reach a successful agreement. What strategies or techniques should he employ to circumvent either or both in order to accomplish that objective?

## Principle Defined and How to Discover It

The term "principle" in this discussion is used in its broadest sense to mean a fundamental truth or motivating force. A person is sometimes referred to as a "man of strict principle." This commonly means that once he has determined that his position is right, whether because of favorable facts, law, or simply because

128

of his own personal convictions or his sense of fair play, he will generally defend it to the bitter end, accepting non-agreement rather than compromise. Winston Churchill expressed it best when he said, "Never give in! Never, Never, Never, Never—in nothing, great or small, large or petty—never give in except to convictions of honour and good sense." [3]

An opposing negotiator or his client may be a "person of strict principle" on any given issue or particular fact pertaining to that issue. It's important for the negotiator to discover this as early in the bargaining as possible in order to fully develop his strategy and techniques to counter-balance it. Otherwise, he may be knocking his head against a brick wall, never really understanding why no progress is being made. Often his opponent will disclose it very early in the bargaining by stating, for example, that he *never* comes in high or low on a valuation issue, but prefers to set a fair price and stick with it until it can be disproved. Or he may be more subtle and say: "My value's fair and I'll stick by it."

On the other hand, probing may be necessary. Questions such as: "Why do you say that? Is there something to support that?" or "Where do you find that?" are all calculated to discover the existence of any applicable principles. An apparent tip-off to the possibility that the opponent or his client is standing firm as a matter of principle may be his reluctance to alter his position on a particular ·fact or issue despite its apparent insignificance. For the most part, however, the existence of principles may often be difficult to detect, and the negotiator should, therefore, always remain on the alert.

## What to Do When Principle Is Involved

The most important point to always bear in mind once it has been determined that a matter of principle is involved, whether it be the opponent's or his client's, is to never directly attack the principle. To do so would be attempting to undermine the very foundation of your opponent's or his client's moral fiber, and thus not only stifle negotiation progress but also run the risk of directly thrusting personality into the discussion.

---

[3] Sir Winston Churchill, Speech at the Harrow School, cited by Dorothy Price and Dean Walley, *Never Give In* (Kansas City: Hallmark Cards Inc.), p. 30.

To illustrate, one evening I happened to tune in on a favorite detective program. A murder had been committed. It seemed that a pretty young girl knew who the murderer was, but stubbornly refused to tell because it would only lead to another death. She said that it was to her a matter of principle. She did not believe that anyone had the right to take the life of another, regardless of what he may have done. The hero, at this point, made a serious blunder—he directly attacked her principle. The result was that tempers flared and communication came to a virtual standstill. Fortunately, however, he made his apologies and everything turned out beautifully.

As I will later point out, personality can stop a negotiation dead in its tracks. The wisest course, when principle is involved, is to attempt to distinguish by facts, law, or other relevant factors why it doesn't apply, or at least to weaken its application to such an extent that the opponent or his client can find it within himself to "give in."

To illustrate, assume that you or your client want to lease certain real estate which will be converted into a large and elegant restaurant. Assume further that the landowner, an elderly lady, is opposed to the sale of either alcohol or tobacco on the premises, particularly to teenagers. It would be a waste of time to attempt to argue the merits (if there are any) of selling alcohol or tobacco to youngsters. That may only serve to reinforce her principle.

A better approach might be to point out that local laws prohibit the sale of such items to minors, or possibly, if the circumstances warrant it, a provision can be placed in the lease prohibiting such sales under certain conditions. Merely stating that most teenagers would not be able to afford to eat at the restaurant because of its high prices may suffice. Whatever the approach, distinguish the principle—don't touch it!

## Personality Defined and How to Discover it

Personality, too, is used here in its broadest sense, to mean an individual's quality of behavior as expressed by his physical and mental activities and attitudes. Personality can and often does creep into every negotiation, no matter how much effort is made to exclude it. People are people, and they will always function at one time or another on an unobjective basis. The trick is to discover when and why.

As I have already stated, the safest rule for the negotiator to follow is to never involve his own personality in the discussion. He must also, however, sharpen his senses to learn to detect when his opponent or his opponent's client has done so. At first glance this may seem easy. Certainly it's fairly elementary to feel the bite of some well-chosen words, see the scowl on an opponent's distorted face, or listen to the sarcastic tone of his voice. All are signs that personality may be involved; but what about those numerous situations where detection may prove very difficult?

For example, a close lawyer friend of mine was negotiating a contract with another lawyer. Progress was difficult for no apparent reason. By chance, my attorney friend finally discovered why. It seemed that the other lawyer had previously had a run-in with an employee of my friend's client, and for some reason lumped everyone into that same basket, including my friend. To avoid such situations and to insure some degree of safety in the preparation of any important negotiation, I always inquire from my client such matters as whether there have been any past dealings with my opponent or his client and, if so, their exact nature. Were they friendly or adverse? Perhaps there were previous legal problems, or maybe an uncollectable account outstanding or litigation. This can often be the case when the client is a large corporation.

## What to Do When Personality Is Involved

Once it has been determined that either the opponent or his client has allowed personality to enter the negotiation, it is important to discover why as early as possible and to directly attempt to eliminate the cause. Bring the facts out into the open. If an apology is in order, make it. If there is a misunderstanding, clear it up. If it is simply a personality conflict, make an honest effort to neutralize it. If your opponent or his client feels that you are making a sincere effort to keep the discussions on an objective basis, in most instances he will respond and cooperate. On the other hand, if he doesn't, you are still well ahead since you have made the effort and are now willing to proceed with full knowledge that personality is involved, and to adapt your strategy and techniques accordingly.

### Principle and Personality

Occasionally, both principle and personality may become simultaneously involved. In such situations, the negotiator should carefully determine and work to overcome the most dominating of the two. His opponent may forego the weaker, particularly if it's personality and he wants to reach a successful agreement on the matter being negotiated. If this can't be accomplished, the negotiator must proceed to dispel even the weaker of the two in order to enhance his chances of success.

# 32

# The Influence of Repetition in Negotiation

My first memorable experience with the use of repetition, oddly enough, occurred when I was a young boy of about eight or nine. As most boys of that age, I used to relish reading comic books of all varieties. One in particular concerned a character called "Captain Marvel," an ordinary individual who, when he uttered a magic word, was transformed into an indestructible foe of crime and injustice. He could fly like superman and brush aside bullets as though they were nothing more than raindrops bouncing off a hard concrete sidewalk.

Having tired of the Captain's constant interference with their dastardly deeds, the villains decided to consult a leading psychologist to assist them in finding a kink in his armour. "It's simple," they were advised. "Call him a weakling. Repeat it enough and he will soon believe it." A campaign was immediately launched and the hero was bombarded with the word "weakling." Leaflets were dropped. Radio ads were aired. Soon everyone began to believe, including the Captain, that he was a weakling. He lost his ability to fly. His arms hung limply at his sides, too heavy, he thought, for him to lift. Things looked very bad.

When a negotiator wishes to emphasize an important point, repetition may serve him well. The mere act of repeating a matter will help insure that his opponent is fully aware of its significance.

133

Timing is important here, as it is in most other instances. Repeating a statement does not mean merely verbatim utterances or utterances without interval, such as was practiced against Captain Marvel. What it means in terms of negotiation is that the *substance* of the matter should be repeated at what the negotiator feels are proper intervals and in the proper context.

For example, assume that the negotiator desires to emphasize the fact that the location of certain agricultural land is perfect for urban development. He might begin by stating just that. Thereafter, he might dwell on such factors as the rapid past growth of the city toward the land in question and that other developed land in the immediate proximity has already been or is about to be annexed into the city. These are forms of repetition designed to accentuate the fact that the land in question is ripe for urban development.

Repetition is excellent for refreshing the opponent's recollection. Often, in lengthy or complex negotiations, important points can be forgotten or lost in the shuffle. Repeating them will therefore greatly assist in minimizing this ever-present danger.

Clarifying a complex or difficult to understand issue can often be done by the simple use of repetition. During the course of the negotiation of a complex matter, I became convinced that the greatest obstacle to success would be to get my opponent to fully comprehend the precise nature of my position. Not that he wasn't a capable person; on the contrary, the difficulty was that the facts were strewn out over a period of several years and not only had to be pieced together like a jigsaw puzzle, but also required the application of both federal and state law. I was fully convinced of the validity of my position. The burden, however, was upon me to demonstrate its soundness to such a degree that it could not be misunderstood. Failing to do so, as Marcus Aurelius once said, I would have to "share the penalty" for my opponent's "mental blindness."

In order to accomplish my objective, I decided to employ repetition as my ally. First, a carefully written summary of the entire matter was set forth in a memorandum. At the next negotiating session my client's issue was clearly reviewed in detail. Any questions were answered and the opponent took extensive notes as the details unfolded. Thereafter, the written memorandum was presented. By this method the entire picture was clearly unmasked. My opponent heard it explained in detail, saw it unfold as he diligently made his own notes, and again had the opportunity to review it in the carefully written memorandum.

There is a caveat here which is illustrated in my foregoing youthful experience. The villians, of course, ultimately failed miserably in their attempt to defeat Captain Marvel because they were endeavoring to use repetition to alter an existing fact, namely, his superhuman strength. Repetition is a positive negotiation technique. Its uses should be confined to reemphasizing important points, refreshing an opponent's recollection, or clarifying difficult or complex situations—*never* to alter existing ones. I know of no quicker and surer way toward failure in any negotiation.

# 33

# *Adding New Elements*

A new element is virtually anything that is foreign to either the subject matter of the negotiation or the parties initially involved in the discussions. Generally speaking, it's unwise to add any new elements because it not only needlessly broadens the discussions but also creates an air of uncertainty. This makes it particularly difficult to control the negotiations and also tends to stifle positive negotiation momentum.

Actually, the negotiator should strive to funnel the discussions toward the desired conclusion. By funneling I mean that, as each point is discussed and agreed upon, it should be set aside unless it's later needed for either review or summation. This process of elimination better enables the negotiator to control the negotiation and to thus reach the desired result.

## What Are New Elements?

Here are several examples of new elements, in order to fully illustrate the point. I've already touched upon interjecting into the discussions new parties other than those initially involved. When this occurs, the opponent generally must reorientate his thinking to the new personality and thus he's liable to raise new thoughts, perhaps even second thoughts, on issues already agreed upon. Bringing in a new party will provide him with the perfect opportunity to do so. Moreover, if the new party is not entirely familiar with what's been previously discussed, he may raise new thoughts on matters already successfully agreed upon and thus inadvertently re-open them for discussion.

Language or even single words may often constitute new elements when not ordinarily used in discussing the particular subject matter involved. Have you ever heard the phrase, "Why, that's criminal?" It crops up occasionally in negotiation. The word "criminal" for most people in our society has a meaning distinctly associated with matters of grave or serious consequences—murder, assault, and robbery, to name only a few. Using it in negotiation, therefore, may easily add a new dimension to the discussions and thus increase the danger of broadening the meaning of the subject matter. Words such as fraud, traitor, or even hypocrite may have a similar effect. All tend to widen the breadth of the discussions and add an air of uncertainty.

New and yet untried methods may often constitute a new element. During the course of arriving at the value of a large parcel of improved real estate, my opponent attempted to use a valuation method that he had developed himself. It provided me with an excellent opportunity to travel all over the waterfront with my inquiries and thus greatly worked to his detriment because he lost complete control of the discussions. Unless the negotiator can cite a reference or authority, he should normally avoid new and untried methods in formal discussions until they have won some degree of acceptance within the particular segment of the public that uses them.

## How to Add New Elements When
## It Becomes Absolutely Essential

Sometimes adding a new element cannot be avoided. When negotiations have reached a standstill, for example, it may become necessary to interject into them something new in order to break the log jam and get matters rolling again. Here's an illustration of how it might be done.

Discussions had been carried on for a considerable length of time with still no success in closing. Numerous parties had previously been involved. I was asked to assist. Recognizing, of course, that my presence would constitute a new element even in a situation such as this, I adopted the following strategy.

The person originally conducting the negotiations and still actively involved was instructed to merely introduce me at the next session and to then commence discussions on his own. It was also suggested that later, as discussions progressed, he dwell on an issue which necessitated an answer or two from me. By this method I was able to gradually work my way into the discussions until eventually I assumed entire control. My presence thus became an acceptable new element.

# 34

# *The Art of Extrapolation*

Extrapolation in its simplest terms means to state logical facts in a manner that can only lead to one inescapable conclusion. Assume you're sitting on the edge of a dock, fishing, and a stranger approaches and asks the proverbial question, "Catch any fish?"

"This is my third carton of bait and I've been here only half an hour," you reply.

Notice that you've merely supplied the stranger with existing pertinent facts from which he must draw the only unmistakable conclusion. The real value of extrapolation then is to allow another to "discover for himself" the desired conclusion.

As you can see, mastering the art can be a very formidable weapon in the negotiator's arsenal of techniques. For one thing, people are much more strongly influenced by their own conclusions. Moreover, an opponent may be much more likely to argue with conclusions advanced by the negotiator as opposed to facts. Hence, if he's simply supplied with the facts and allowed to draw his own conclusions, he is obviously not going to question his own judgment. Extrapolation is thus a very effective form of demonstration.

Men beware if the little woman masters this technique. Note the following conversation.

Harry: "My shirts look terrible, Gladys! What have you been doing to them, anyway?"

Gladys (innocently): "I don't know what's wrong, Harry. I used the same powder, the same amount of water and water temperature, and washed them the same length of time." (Notice that she's making it unmistakably clear what the culprit is.)

Harry: "Looks like the machine just isn't doing the job anymore." (Ah! He's taken the bait.)

Gladys: "I think you're right, Harry. It must be the washing machine." (She's extrapolated. He's concluded. She's reinforced his conclusion. I wonder if she's enhanced her odds of getting a new washing machine?)

To take an illustration more conducive to formal negotiation, assume you're negotiating the sale of a business and your opponent asks, "What is the future profit potential?" You could, of course, give him your opinion or the opinions of other knowledgeable persons. But why not extrapolate? Let him draw his own conclusion as to what the future holds. Here's how it might be done:

"Sales have increased an average of ten per cent annually over the past five years or fifty per cent, and net profits fifteen per cent per year or seventy-five per cent over the same period. In addition, the company has two new products that have been selling very well which are expected to add favorably to both sales net profits."

By drawing upon existing logical facts as to past performance and calling them to the attention of your opponent, isn't it fair to assume that he will inescapably conclude that the future profit potential looks good? Again, never lose sight of the fact that people are much more strongly influenced by conclusions that they feel *they* have arrived at *themselves*. To extrapolate, then, is to employ a very effective technique, one that is extremely pursuasive and designed to make a point with much more impact and finesse. As long as your opponent feels that he is making the decisions, you should make excellent negotiation progress!

# 35

# *The Question Method*

There are numerous advantages to posing questions during the course of any negotiation. Questions can be excellent probing tools to discover additional facts and other information that may only be known to an opponent or otherwise extremely difficult for the negotiator to discover. In addition, they can offer the negotiator more of an assurance of control over the negotiations and may be useful in putting the opponent on the defensive. Attacking the opponent's positions by well timed and phrased questions can often pay rich dividends, and nothing can be more indispensable to cast doubt upon an opponent's position than a timely question.

**General and Specific Questions**

General questions are useful for probing and are best during the early stages of negotiation. As matters unfold, however, it is usually better to refrain from asking them in order not to run the danger of reopening already agreed upon items, or to unfavorably' reflect upon the negotiator's thoroughness of preparation or grasp of the subject matter. In addition, a wise opponent may be able to detect when the negotiator is attempting to strengthen his own knowledge by general questions, and his responses may therefore not be too enlightening.

Specific questions are much safer to venture out with, since they call for fairly confined answers. They're useful in any phase of the negotiation, but more so in the latter stages when the negotiator is more apt to know precisely what he is after when asking. (It goes without saying that there should always be an objective at the end of every question, whether it be general or specific. Asking merely to be asking or to satisfy curiosity is never to be recommended. Often a skillful opponenet may attempt to build up a situation simply for the purpose of drawing out a particular question in order to provide himself with an ideal opportunity to let go with a very damaging or perhaps even devastating reply. I've already indicated, in the section titled *Why It's Important to Determine Who Has Final Negotiating Authority*, how my opponent fell into this trap even though his question had a specific objective.)

Whether a question is general or specific, it should be carefully phrased and descriptive in order to have the greatest impact. Descriptive questions will provide the opponent with more of a mental picture of the answer to be elicited. Contrast "Where is the property located?" with "Is the property located near transportation, adequate labor supplies and ample utilities?" The latter question is obviously more illustrative of the negotiator's objectives and thus more likely to draw a productive response. In addition, being a more specific question, it doesn't permit the opponent to ride all over the range with his response and perhaps be evasive or even seize the offensive.

Following are some of the more useful varieties of questions to any negotiator.

## Leading Questions

Leading questions are excellent for maintaining control of the negotiation and facilitating continuity in the negotiator's train of thought. A leading question is simply a statement turned into a question, and is designed to draw a favorable response by a "yes" or "no" or other short answer. That's one major reason why they are very good in maintaining control. It's essential, therefore, for the negotiator to know or to have a reasonably good idea of the answer to the question before he asks it. Otherwise, it no longer becomes a leading question, but one that may be leading him into areas that he may not desire to tread.

"It's a very profitable company, isn't it?" or "He was traveling very fast, wasn't he?" are two examples of leading questions. Both could have just as easily been turned around to:

"It's a very profitable company!" and "He was traveling very fast!" By adding the "isn't it" and "wasn't he" or similar phrases, however, the statements were converted into questions that called for an affirmative response from the opponent. Thus, the most important function of a leading question is to draw from an opponent an answer most favorable to the negotiator.

## Suggestive Questions

As the name implies, a suggestive question is one that incorporates or suggests a specific course of action within the question. For example, "Don't you agree that the value presents fairly the fair market value?" or "Don't you think it's better to execute both copies now?" In both cases the opponent must commit himself to either the course of action suggested in the question or explain why not. These questions are common in life and a favorite in the retailing business. How many times have you gone into a department store to buy a new shirt only to have an alert store employee inquire, "How about a new tie or a pair of cufflinks to go with it?" Contrast this with a leading question, which as you recall, is actually a statement turned into a question. "You can use a tie or cufflinks to go with that, can't you?" The former is a pure question which is suggestive in nature, whereas the latter is a statement turned into a question.

A leading question is more a bullying type of question and may cause some resentment in situations such as this. The suggestive question technique is therefore much more suitable.

## Questions That Call For Obvious Answers

These questions are very similar to leading questions. The primary distinction, however, is that these are designed to elicit a response favorable to the negotiator because the opponent doesn't want to make himself appear unknowledgeable or ignorant even though he may actually not have personal knowledge of the correct answer. Questions of this type should normally be confined to matters that are of common knowledge (even though they may be in specialized areas). "Doesn't everyone know that building costs have changed?" or simply, "Don't we all know this?" or "Isn't it well that everyone accepts it as a fact?" are examples. As earlier indicated, all are designed to get an opponent to agree, even though he may not be certain of the correct answer. He simply may not be inclined to buck the general trend of opinion.

These types of questions can be useful in many facets of negotiation. For example, during the course of a negotiation on a federal estate tax matter, one of the issues centered around the value of common stock in what was then a closely held corporation. The valuation date in any estate is the date of death (assuming the alternate date has not been selected), and only those circumstances existing on the date of death may be considered in arriving at the value of any asset in the estate. Subsequent to the date of death the stock was sold for a considerably higher value. The entire circumstance surrounding the sale, however, occurred after the date of death. In other words, on the date of death there was absolutely no indication in any manner that the stock would be sold.

In order to get the government to acknowledge this fact, the following question was asked: "Isn't it a fact that only those circumstances existing on the date of death can be considered?" The response, of course, was "Yes." Thereafter, by producing a letter from the purchaser of the stock which specifically indicated that the initial contact for purchasing the stock occurred after the date of death, it was a much simpler matter to convince my opponent that the value of the stock was the value returned by the estate rather than the much higher value paid for by the subsequent purchaser. My "obvious answer question" became the lead-in or foundation on which the entire later discussions were based.

## Questions That Require a Choice

An opponent may often attempt evasive tactics on matters that the negotiator wants to button down. Choice questions can be a good technique to pin him down. The negotiator should know precisely the choices before asking the question, and both should preferably be favorable to him. "Would you prefer to use the gross income method of determining value on the property, or a multiple of net income?" "Would you prefer to discuss blockage on the basis of a per share price or gross value?" are illustrations. For the lady of the house bargaining, perhaps, for some new furniture: "Would you prefer to give me that sofa and chair for seven hundred dollars, or those two over there for five hundred and fifty?"

## Successive Questions

These questions are excellent for maintaining control and developing positive and forceful negotiation momentum. Assume, for example, that the negotiator is attempting to get a rental reduction on a prospective lease. Here's how the successive question technique might unfold. The questions are stated in rapid succession in order not to allow time for an answer by an opponent until the final question has been posed. Hopefully, by that time the answer can only be the one sought by the negotiator:

"Why is it high? Why is it unreasonable? Isn't competition down the street leasing similar space for 20 per cent less? Why, then, should someone pay more? Is there something in addition to the space being offered? I've looked at it; what can it be? Is there? Perhaps I'm wrong? Am I? If not, wouldn't it seem reasonable for us to pay a sum for the space similar to what we can get elsewhere?"

## Successive Questions with Answers

By this technique the negotiator intersperses his own well-thought-out answers with his questions. It not only maintains control but also makes it difficult for the opponent to say "no." Using the same rental reduction example, the method might look like this. Here again, rapid succession of both the questions and answers is necessary, without an opportunity for the opponent to respond until the final answer:

"Why is it high? Why is it unreasonable? Because your competition down the street will lease us similar space for 20 per cent less! Why should we pay more? Is there something in addition to the space being offered? I've gone through the property

carefully and there certainly doesn't seem to be! In fact, it seems
to be fairly identical! Perhaps we're wrong? If so, please advise us.
Otherwise, it would seem that the amount we're willing to pay is
quite reasonable—a fair return for the lessor and a reasonable
outlay by the lessee!"

## Conclusion

In concluding this section, the reader should be fully aware
of the fact that questions and their effectiveness in any negotiation are directly proportionate to the negotiator's experience in
using them. Accordingly, learn to use them frequently and, if
necessary, even write them out beforehand until they become
second nature. Only in this manner can they become useful
servants.

# 36

# *The Art of Flowing Through*

Flowing through in negotiation, in essence, means to take the path of least resistance. In most negotiations of any importance there will often come a time when the parties have reached a standstill on a particular point or issue. When this occurs, it's important for the negotiator to learn to flow with the discussion, working to maintain an atmosphere of compatability and momentum in order to insure negotiation progress. By mastering the art of flowing through he may have just the technique to either prevent or break the log jam and to get matters flowing freely again.

For example, if there are a great many issues to be negotiated and a standstill has been reached on one or more, going on to the less controversial and allowing the others to cool off is a good way to maintain positive momentum. This may also often result in even settling those that are of a controversial nature, particularly if they are few in number. By wrapping up all of the others, the parties are much more apt to reach an agreement on any sticky one remaining in order to close out the entire matter. Conversely, dwelling on a matter that appears to be at a point of nonagreeability may lead to forfeiture of agreements on numerous other, less controversial points or issues that would otherwise be readily agreed to.

Note that the point or matter on which the parties have reached a standstill need not necessarily be a full-blown controversy. On the contrary, the art of flowing through can be useful to advance the negotiator's position in almost every conceivable situation. To illustrate, during the course of a negotiation, my opponent declined to discuss some of the issues because he said that he had not had ample time to prepare. Being fully prepared myself, I wanted to proceed with as many as possible. I therefore suggested that he look over the issues now with the thought that some were perhaps of a nature that could be readily agreed upon without further preparation. He concurred, and several were quickly settled.

Obviously, it would have been unwise to attempt to get my opponent to negotiate on the issues when he wasn't prepared. On the other hand, I did not desire that my valuable preparation time on these issues go completely unrewarded. Thus, by following the path of least resistance—issues on which there may not be any serious disagreement—negotiation progress was sustained.

Flowing through also means that when discussions may have reached a snag, and it becomes absolutely necessary to unravel it before any progress can be made, the negotiator should strive to undo the easiest parts of the knot first. Again, this is merely following the path of least resistance. This will bring the parties back on to some semblance of common ground from which work can begin on the tighter, more difficult parts.

Finally, the negotiator should learn to readily agree to points that are of no consequence. Remember that controversy impedes progress. By flowing through on such minor items, he will thus not only be conveying to his opponent the need for concentration only on points or issues of substance and thus avoiding the danger of controversy on such smaller matters, but also projecting a no-nonsense, business-like image that facilitates negotiation progress.

# 37

# *Emotional Appeal*

*"Persuasion may come through the hearers, when
the speech stirs their emotions."*
Aristotle

Appealing to the emotions is an age-old practice. All of us are
a bundle of emotions. Pride, fear, anger, sorrow, joy and shame, to
name only a few, lie dormant within us, waiting for the right
stimulant to arouse them. Once they're aroused we're motivated
toward action.

Most of us are very familiar with what happens when a
person becomes emotionally involved. Inwardly, it's very difficult,
if not impossible, to describe what takes place when, for example,
a person experiences the negative emotion of sorrow. Outwardly,
however, all we need to see is perhaps the downcast expression
and the tears, or hear the sorrowful wail to know that there's
sadness around.

We are not so much concerned here with the complexity
surrounding the psychological aspects of emotions and their effect
upon a person. That's not essential to employing emotional appeal
in negotiation. What is essential is knowledge of what may trigger
them and how that knowledge may be utilized to the negotiator's
best advantage. Because emotions play such an important role in
everything else in life, it's self-evident that they can likewise take
the spotlight in negotiation.

There are essentially three separate areas that will have a tremen-
dously strong impact upon an opponent's emotions. One is *wealth*,
which includes money and any other form of real or personal

property that an opponent attaches value to. A second is *recognition,* which in negotiation means essentially an opponent who is greatly desirous of having others recognize him for his appearance or accomplishments, or both. The third is *self-preservation,* the desire to be safe and secure. The degree to which the desire for wealth, recognition, and self-preservation will affect the emotions varies between individuals. Some would rather have wealth than the other two. Others would much prefer recognition. Perhaps they already have wealth or are too old to enjoy it. For others, the greatest appeal may lie in self-preservation.

Let's examine each one separately and see how each fits into negotiation and how the negotiator may employ each to his advantage. Before we do that, however, let me make one final but very important point. When a person becomes emotionally involved, he may often bypass a meticulous consideration of matters that would ordinarily call for it. He is thus substituting an emotional judgment for a judgment based upon the merits.

Appealing to the emotions is thus a separate form of persuasion. Therein lies its real worth. If the negotiator's position is weak on merits, he can swing to appealing to the emotions or perhaps employ a combination of both.

## Appealing to the Emotions Through Wealth

I read recently in a newspaper that the great American dream is to become an instant millionaire. For some that may be true; for others, perhaps not. Whichever the case, one thing is certain. Most have a very strong desire for wealth and the security and independence that go with it. Wealth will pay the doctor and hospital bills. It will purchase plenty of travel and the most expensive braces for the kid's teeth. It'll also provide tremendous power. Some want it solely for that purpose.

Most matters of negotiation concern wealth in one form or another. It follows that wealth is a very fertile area of emotional appeal. Whenever the negotiator can demonstrate to his opponent how going along with the negotiator's proposals will either add to the opponent's wealth or preserve his existing wealth, he's adopted a sound strategy—provided, of course, that wealth is his opponent's strongest emotional appeal.

As I've already related, wealth in this discussion includes all forms of property in addition to money so long as the opponent attaches some value to it. To illustrate, one person may consider an old windmill to be a piece of junk and thus attach little or no value to it. So if you're negotiating the sale of a farm, it would undoubtedly concern your opponent very little to learn that a windmill comes with the purchase. Another may consider the windmill to be a real antique, however, and have a real need for it, perhaps to add character to the farm or even to sell it through his antique dealership or put it in front of a new restaurant as a gimmick to attract customers. To him it has a great deal of value and thus either gaining or losing it may easily trigger an emotional response. He thus may not particularly concern himself with such matters as the quality of the land for producing crops or its location convenience.

I purposely selected this far-out windmill example not only to illustrate the need for an opponent to attach value to it, but also to show that value can vary disproportionately between individuals, even in relation to the entire value of the subject matter of negotiation. The farm is certainly worth more than the windmill, but the opponent may already own a thousand acres. What's a hundred or two more? He thus may place greater emotional value on the windmill, and the thought of either gaining or losing it will motivate him toward positive action. .

## Appealing to the Emotions Through Recognition

Recognition is one of the strongest sources of emotional appeal. We've already learned of the importance that a person places upon his "self." The desire for recognition will sometimes propel a person to go to great lengths to achieve it. The degree of this desire varies between individuals. Most of us think well of ourselves and take care to dress and act properly. We're very concerned with not only how we see ourselves and how we would like others to see us, but also how others actually look upon us.

Wearing flashy clothes, wigs, driving elegant cars, arriving late at public functions so others will know they're there, talking loudly to focus attention upon themselves and even committing crimes, sometimes serious ones, in order to see their name in print, all point toward a strong desire for recognition in some people.

The same is true of initialed cuff links and tie clasps, and even monogrammed shirts and ties. I once negotiated a matter where, after signing his name to several preliminary documents, my opponent wrote in his title after his signature. It was an immediate tip-off to his strong desire for recognition.

Once the negotiator learns that recognition is his opponent's strongest desire, he virtually has him at his mercy. Those who really crave recognition will generally take whatever risks are necessary to achieve it. By framing his proposals to either satisfy that craving or to keep from depriving him of it, the negotiator's task will become that much easier. In a later section I point out how suggesting that a press conference be held to announce an agreement greatly motivated my opponent. I was appealing directly to his sense of recognition. There are, of course, numerous other means. Some may be more subtle.

For instance, assume you're negotiating the settlement of a controversy surrounding an employment contract. The employee, a former top executive and very prominent in business circles, was discharged. He contends that the discharge was wrongful and that he should be entitled to all of the benefits of his contract. The company, on the other hand, refuses to pay the full amount, claiming that he was discharged in accordance with a provision in the contract that allowed discharge in the event the Board of Directors felt that he was not properly performing the responsibilities of his position.

This form of dispute is fairly common and can often lead to bitter controversy. With the thousands of companies and the innumerable types of executives that they employ, there's a constant flux of key personnel. Sometimes the discharge is based upon merit. Other times the motives can range anywhere from personalities to even nepotism. Without subscribing a motive to our example, one of the ways to appeal to the employee's desire for recognition is to point out to him that there are no animosities involved and that the company will be happy to recommend him highly to other potential employers. This will keep intact his reputation in the business community and thus not destroy the years of hard work that went into building it. Another way is to indicate that in any public announcements, whether they be newspapers, television, or business or trade magazines, he will be spoken of highly.

Both approaches are designed to prevent the employee from losing recognition. If he's the type of person that places the desire for it on a high pedestal, the likelihood of reaching a favorable settlement will thus be greatly increased.

## Appealing to the Emotions Through Self-Preservation

Just as some people's greatest desire is wealth or the need to be recognized, still others afford the number one spot to the desire not to be harmed. Thus, anything that tends to insure their self-preservation will stimulate a favorable emotional response. Anything that threatens it will reverse that response.

Again, it's important to bear in mind that self-preservation is not restricted to the individual person, but includes virtually everything he considers a part of his self. This takes in his home, relatives, friends, organizations that he belongs to, together with numerous other matters that are all a part of him. The closer the endangered matter is to his self, the greater the emotional response.

To take a simple everyday illustration, assume you're a home owner and you call in a repairman to fix a leaky garage roof. Looking the job over, he advises you that what's really needed is a complete new roof. If the garage is old and outdated, it might be difficult to convince you to go to the expense. But what if you use the garage for storing family heirlooms, trophies or other paraphernalia which, although possessing no great extrinsic value, are very dear to you and your family. You might be inclined to go for the new roof. And if the repairman is wise enough to sense your attachment to them and thus the need for their self-preservation, he'd make his pitch on that basis. By merely pointing out the harm that will come to them from the water, he can force you to respond emotionally. And the bleaker the picture he can paint, the greater your emotional response.

Sometimes the need for self-preservation can completely stifle negotiation progress. If, for example, a union's demands are so high that they would force the company to walk a financial tightrope, perhaps even put it out of business, there's no way the company will agree to them. To do so would endanger its very competitive existance. Likewise, any position that a negotiator advances which endangers an opponent's self-preservation will be met with similar resistance. It's important, therefore, for the negotiator to always consider his proposals in this light.

Occasionally a negotiator will adopt the strategy that he doesn't particularly care whether any of his proposals will endanger his opponent's self-preservation, his thinking being that if he takes an extreme position, regardless of its consequences, he can back off whenever he meets with resistance and thus ultimately end up with a much better agreement. The fallacy of this approach is that in actual practice it can and often does backfire. Frequently an opponent will simply shut off discussions, particularly if the danger to his self-preservation is great enough. If he senses that the negotiator is deliberately attempting this strategy, he'll be very apt to question his sincerity on all of the positions that he's advancing.

This approach can actually be a form of "creating" the desire for self-preservation. High demands are deliberately made in order to trigger an emotional response toward self-preservation because of the threatened security. Then, by backing off or lowering the demands, the threat to security is relieved, thereby prompting an emotional response in order to preserve it. The person experiencing the emotions may thus give in on matters he would have ordinarily resisted.

I don't recommend this technique and only mention it here in order to make the reader aware of its existence. If you sense it is being used, straighten the matter out quickly by threatening to break off the discussions. This can often be the perfect approach to triggering an emotional response from the other side, particularly if he has a strong desire for wealth, recognition, or self-preservation, and the subject matter of the negotiation will satisfy any of them.

# 38

# Silence

Silence enhances one's authority.
Winston Churchill

Even a fool, when he holdeth his peace, is counted wise: and he that shutteth his lips is esteemed a man of understanding.

PROVERBS 17:28

Only the amateur fears to be silent for a moment lest interest lag. He depends solely on words to capture attention. The artful performer knows that rhythm patterns require silence too, and nothing is more dramatic and effective than a long motionless pause after a statement. It permits absorption of the thought. It permits reflection. But more important, it compels attention to what has been said as if an italicized finger had been pointed at it.[4]
Louis Nizer

---

[4] Louis Nizer, THINKING ON YOUR FEET (New York: Pyramid Publications, Inc., 1963), p. 26.

# 39

# *The Warmth of a Smile*

Never underestimate the strength of a friendly smile. I recall when I was a young army recruit and it was my turn to be on the receiving end of the classical tongue lashing from the company's first sergeant. As he stood there on the podium glaring down at me, a broad smile was firmly fixed upon his slender face. It somehow mellowed his remarks (which I won't repeat here) and made them a little more digestible.

When you greet your opponent for the first time, you should do so with a warm, genuine smile. Its effects can be magical. Your smile is telling him that you are pleased to see him, and even though the anticipated subject of discussion may be difficult or perhaps even controversial, you are prepared to approach it on an objective basis. The same applies when you're departing. Even if the negotiation has been hard, perhaps with tempers becoming involved, resist the temptation to show displeasure. A warm smile will again show your objectiveness and can even pave the way toward more negotiating progress.

It's happened on numerous occasions. I can recall one in particular where I advised my opponent that his position was unacceptable and that it was our intention of exercising other avenues open to us. I thanked him for his time, and with a friendly smile to let him know that there were no ill feelings, bid him farewell. The reaction was immediate. He seemed to be reluctant to leave, as though drawn back by my smile, and finally again asked why his position wasn't acceptable. We discussed the matter further and reached a successful agreement.

A pleasant negotiating atmosphere is conducive to progress. A warm, genuine smile will help provide that atmosphere. If harsh words should become necessary, that doesn't mean that the negotiator should spend the remainder of the session with a sour look upon his face. Keep it there only as long as it is necessary to make your point, then discard it. Your opponent will appreciate the change. It's a good way of letting him know that you will not hesitate to get tough if necessary, but that you're not going to let it dominate the entire discussion and thus stifle progress.

Let me emphasize that I am not advocating that a negotiator go through a negotiation with a smile fixed rigidly upon his face. That's obviously unrealistic, in addition to very poor taste and tactics. Let your facial expressions flow naturally, but never lose sight of the fact that a friendly, genuine smile is an essential part of human contact. It's never a sign of weakness, but rather one of sincerity and interest in your fellow man—your opponent. Use it! He'll appreciate it and respond accordingly.

# 40

# Disposing of Potentially Troublesome Arguments

Here we are concerned with arguments or contentions advanced by an opponent that have not yet fully bloomed but may very well do so unless nipped early in the proceedings. Sometimes these arguments or contentions may be of little substance as far as the subject matter of the negotiation is. concerned, but if allowed to gain momentum they may very easily become troublesome.

The most important point to always bear in mind is to never lend weight to them. This may often be done inadvertently. Spending considerable time in discussion or preparing lengthy memoranda to refute a point may easily tend to leave the impression that it's of much greater significance than may first appear. On the other side of the coin, one or two carefully worded sentences may have an opposite effect.

Key words can often do more to squelch potentially troublesome arguments than virtually anything else. I've already stressed the importance of the negotiator's language. Here's where it can really pay dividends! Phrases such as: "I see little merit ... " or "It's routine ... " or even "It's a simple, well-established practice ... " are all designed to minimize the importance of a position.

To take a simple, everyday illustration, assume you've had some work done on your home and the contractor failed to use the materials specified in the contract. When he comes to collect, you refuse to pay unless either the right materials are installed or the price is reduced to compensate for the substitute. After all, you argue, why should I pay the contract price for something I don't really want? The contractor counters with the argument, among others, that the quality of the materials used is comparable to those specified. This, of course, can be a very troublesome argument if allowed to fully develop. Following are several ways in which it might be handled.

You can say, "Prove it," of course, but that would only serve to challenge him to assimilate data to support his position. Once he's gone that far it will be very unlikely that he'll agree to any price reduction. You can indicate, "That still doesn't mean that I have to pay the contract price for something I didn't want!" It's a little stronger, but still not designed to dispose of the argument. Rather, it allows it to linger on and perhaps continue to grow in stature. Finally, you can reply, "The quality of the material is specified in our contract, and that's the *only* one I've agreed to pay for." This response shuts off his argument almost completely. It says to the contractor's contention, in effect: "So what! It's not what you've installed but what the contract calls for that's controlling."

From what I've said, it's apparent that the negotiator must consider each argument raised by an opponent very carefully before responding. Most often this must be done in the heat of battle, with little time to contemplate. As each proposal is made or an argument is raised, he must develop the ability to quickly run through the alternate responses within himself, and to just as quickly come up with the right one. It's a good way to eliminate many potentially troublesome arguments and thus save a lot of headaches down the road.

When the negotiator has time to contemplate an argument, he can, of course, reach his approach with greater care. It may therefore be better, in some instances, to ask for time to "think the matter over." But this, too, can inadvertently add emphasis to an otherwise weak position, since an opponent may tend to think that his contention is strong enough to warrant more serious consideration. Consequently, the better practice in most instances is to develop the ability to quickly and efficiently take apart each argument right on the spot and play down those that you may not want to allow to fully bloom.

# 41

# Building Goodwill

When I was an agent with the U. S. Treasury Department, during the course of an audit I discovered an asset that had been inadvertently omitted from the tax return. The taxpayer's representative became somewhat disturbed at the thought of paying an increased tax. When I pointed out, however, that the value placed on the asset would be his new tax basis (the value used in computing taxable gain or loss upon sale) which could either cut down on any gain in the event the asset is sold at a higher figure or entitle the taxpayer to a loss if sold for less, his resistance melted away.

## What is Goodwill

Goodwill in negotiation simply means doing your opponent a favor. In my above experience I pointed out legal benefits accruing to the taxpayer. There are numerous other ways. In all, however, there is an important limitation attached. By doing the favor *it must not be detrimental in any manner to the negotiator's position.* Notice that pointing out legal benefits that the taxpayer was entitled to if he went along with inclusion of the asset at my value did not detract from my position, but actually, enhanced my chances of success. Negotiation, as I've already indicated on numerous occasions, is generally a freewheeling affair with no guidelines to work from. It's not the negotiator's responsibility to help win his opponent's case. The favors that you do for him, therefore, must never, in any way, shape or form, adversely effect your negotiating position.

161

## Why It Is Necessary to Build Goodwill

Skillful negotiation requires that the negotiator build a bridge of trust between himself and his opponent. It also requires that an opponent be motivated toward making decisions favorable to the negotiator. Both are directly related to your opponent's frame of mind.

Doing him a favor is one of the best ways of putting him in the right frame of mind. If he feels that he can trust you, even though you may be hard-hitting at the bargaining table, you can be sure that your task will be just that much easier. Each favor that you do for him builds a plank in that bridge of trust. It'll motivate him, just as it did with my opponent in the above experience. In fact, in that experience it motivated him so much that he later called to again thank me for pointing out the tax benefits that may later legally flow to his client, because it made his unpleasant task of telling his client that he'd have to pay additional taxes much easier.

Another benefit of building goodwill is that it pays dividends whenever you later have the occasion (which may occur often) to negotiate with the same opponent on a new matter. He will remember the favor that you did for him the last time. And if he doesn't, tactfully refresh his recollection.

## How To Build Goodwill

Now that we know what goodwill is and why it's necessary, let's turn our attention to the various means of building it. Our first method, a simple one—apprising our opponent of benefits he was legally entitled to—worked well. There are others that are equally effective.

A good one is pointing out errors that may adversely affect him. For example, recently an opponent submitted some financial statements that he had prepared from which an asset had been inadvertently omitted. By disclosing the error, did I violate the important limitation that the favor must not be detrimental to my position? Let's look at it more closely. It was fully understood by all of the parties that the asset would be included in the purchase and we were negotiating on that basis. In attempting to arrive at the value, one of the sources of reference was the financial statements. There were others, however, and the error would certainly be picked up. By disclosing it as soon as it was discovered, it warmed up my opponent considerably since he'd prepared them, and thus a plank was laid in the bridge of trust between us.

Still another good way is by making suggestions that may be helpful in the event the negotiations are successfully concluded. These can be made during the discussions and may tend to actually facilitate a successful agreement as a matter of planned strategy in addition to building goodwill. I once suggested a press conference to announce a closed agreement. It was a natural follow through to a matter that I felt the public would appreciate learning about. My opponent (a person whom I came to greatly respect) was pleased with the suggestion and acted upon it.

Another more common example of this method might be a situation involving the purchase of a pet. Assume you are an avid sportsman and have decided to buy several dogs to be trained for hunting purposes. You hope to have them compete in the various competitive field trials and are hopeful of success. By pointing this out to your opponent (the seller) and indicating that any resulting publicity for the dogs may benefit his kennels, you have enhanced your chances of making a favorable purchase.

# 42

# *Use of Demonstrative Exhibits*

By demonstrative exhibits I am referring to any evidence that has a direct effect upon an opponent with little or no necessity for any oral discussion, except perhaps for an explanation as to its relevance. It includes such items as photographs, moving pictures, pamphlets, mechanical apparatus, art work, diagrams on blackboards, and anything else that requires visual inspection. People tend to place much more credibility upon what they see than what they hear. Demonstrative evidence, therefore, can play a significant part in any negotiation.

If I were to describe a waterfall, it might be difficult for the listener to really get a picture of the scene unless he had either a vivid and lively imagination or I was extremely good with my description. But if I were to show him a color picture of the falls or, better yet, moving pictures showing the cascading water, with tiny beads drifting skyward to form a beautiful rainbow as they are penetrated by the sun's warm rays, it would be easy to see. Demonstrative evidence thus transmits the desired objective very quickly and effectively.

Another of its important functions is to dramatize a particular situation. It's one thing to describe the use of an artificial leg and entirely another to drop it on the table and say: "Here's what this person is going to have to walk with for the rest of his life," or, "How would you like to spend the rest of your life jogging around on this?" The full significance of what the negotiator is trying to demonstrate is brought home with such great impact that it may sometimes actually swing the preponderance in his favor.

Demonstrative evidence serves the additional function of freeing the mind for concentration on other matters and, in addition, greatly assists in assuring accuracy, a quality the negotiator should always take pains to promote.

Take, for instance, a corporate balance sheet. In the usual situation it would be unwise to attempt to commit any significant portions of it to memory. It's generally loaded with useful information and answers literally dozens of questions, such as: What is the cost of fixed assets? How much depreciation has been taken? How much cash does the corporation have? What are its long term liabilities? How many shares of stock and what classes are authorized and outstanding? Why not use it in the negotiation unless there are compelling reasons not to? It'll free the mind and insure complete accuracy.

Recently I went into a smart little shop that sold, among other things, Oriental incense and candles. It would have been very difficult to accurately describe the various sweet-smelling odors that could come from them. But as soon as the saleslady lit a few, there could be no mistaking their pleasant fragrance.

On some occasions demonstrative evidence can provide fresh insight into a difficult problem, and can often supply enough of a push to get the negotiation over the hill and heading on a downgrade toward an easier road to success. I was engaged in a complex negotiation, made more cumbersome because there was very little in the way of direct factual evidence to support my client's position. The matter centered around a public institution whose size I wanted to emphasize. After constant and careful digging, I finally came upon several printed and illustrated brochures, the type that are sometimes distributed to the public. These were given to my opponent at an appropriate time during the discussions and very effectively accomplished my objective.

There is still another thought on the use of demonstrative evidence that the negotiator should always keep before him whenever considering its use. If it is an essential part of his case, he should strive to keep it within the visibility of his opponent throughout most, if not all, of the negotiation. Refer to it during the discussion if interest in it seems to lag. The longer an opponent looks at it, the more convincing and formidable it becomes, until its eventual effect can be quite devastating in terms of favorable results.

Finally, it goes without saying that there should always be a definite objective in using this type of evidence. Be absolutely certain that it can help you. If you're sitting on the middle of the fence as to its usefulness, it's better not to use it. If it can't help you, it can only hurt you. Moreover, as I touched upon earlier, its impact can be very strong, and it's often the type of evidence that an opponent will not be likely to forget.

# 43

# *Making the Offer or Counter-Offer*

An offer is a proposal to do a thing. Sometimes it's oral and sometimes it's in writing. When the lady of the house, for example, shops at the supermarket, she generally finds the shelves stacked neatly with hundreds of items, all with prices stamped on them. The grocer is making her an offer to sell at those prices. When she pays the cashier, she signifies her acceptance and the deal is closed.

If, on the other hand, she says she'll take the steak (she's satisfied with the quality, size, etc.) but wants it for five cents less per pound, she's making a counter-offer. A counter-offer is a reply to an offer which adds qualifications to the offer or requires performance of new conditions not expressed in the offer. The counter-offer amounts to non-acceptance of the offer, and, in turn, must be accepted to become binding. The store owner or manager (the cashier probably doesn't have the authority) can either accept the counter-offer, make a counter-offer of his own, or renew his original offer.

The foregoing supermaket principles apply to any negotiation, regardless of its size and complexity.

## Some Essential Guidelines

In most instances it is best to state clearly the basis or reasons for any offer or counter-offer. It does little good to make an offer

167

or counter-offer if an opponent is not made fully aware of the reasons for it. How else can he determine whether it's reasonable?

It's generally best to set a time limit on any offer or counter-offer. It will not only be more likely to prompt some action on the part of the opponent and perhaps create some anxiety on his part, particularly if he wants to reach an agreement badly enough, but it will also allow the negotiator to more fully formulate his own plans.

Never develop a reputation of coming in high or low with offers or counter-offers. It's far better, I've found, to come in with a proposal well supported by the facts, law and other circumstances. This puts a greater burden upon an opponent, since he knows that he will have to come up with some pretty convincing evidence to refute the negotiator's position.

Be a good listener. When the other side is making an offer or counter-offer, be absolutely certain that you understand it fully. If not, never hesitate to ask questions. Nothing can be more damaging than to find out that what was thought to be the terms of a proposal later turn out to be something else.

Avoid polarization. "I will never" or "Absolutely not" or similar unbending utterances tend to isolate the negotiator. Change is the only thing constant in life and this applies doubly in negotiation. New facts and other circumstances often arise that may require a change of position, and if the negotiator has painted himself into a corner by such phrases, he may be depriving himself of the desired flexibility.

Whenever an offer or counter-offer is rejected, never become angry. Remember, the burden is always upon the negotiator to demonstrate the merits of his position, and the first place he should look if he hasn't reached a favorable agreement is to himself—so remain cool.

## Who Makes the Initial Offer

No firm rule exists as to who should make the offer. Generally, however, the person who institutes the negotiation should be prepared to make an offer. It's important for the negotiator to understand that if he is going to make the initial offer, he should be certain that he knows precisely what it will be and why. Otherwise, he should not venture out until he has fully satisfied himself as to these important aspects. A counter-offer, as earlier indicated, is merely a varied proposal to an offer or another counter-offer. The same importance, however, should be attached to it, the negotiator knowing precisely what it will be and why.

In some complex negotiations the offers and counter-offers sometimes run into the dozens. Here, again, each time a change is made it is important to call the opponent's attention to the reasons for it. The more the negotiator is able to justify the basis for his offer or counter-offer, the greater the chance of acceptance.

In many negotiations it's better to have an opponent make the initial offer. Assume, for example, that the owner of real estate is approached by an interested purchaser. Even if the owner knows what he would like to get for the property, it might be wiser for him to let the interested purchaser make the initial offer, since he may want the property badly enough to go much higher than the owner might normally expect. To illustrate, here are some examples.

*POOR STRATEGY*

Opponent: "How much do you want for the property?"
Negotiator: "In the area of seventy-five thousand dollars."
(The owner has committed himself and the top value has now been set.)

*BETTER STRATEGY*

Opponent: "How much do you want for the property?"
Negotiator: "How much are you willing to pay?"
(This approach puts the burden upon the purchaser, but still allows him to come in lower in order to feel out or fence with the owner.)

*BEST STRATEGY*

Opponent: "How much do you want for the property?"
Negotiator: "You said you wanted to buy. I didn't say I wanted to sell."
(This puts the burden heavily upon the purchaser. In most instances he'll come with a more realistic figure in order to make it more attractive to the owner.)

# 44

# *Setting a Precedent*

An important consideration in any negotiation is whether any of the positions that the negotiator advances or the agreements that he makes will be binding in the future. This likelihood is generally present whenever future negotiations will be carried on involving one or more of the same parties or the same or similar issues, whether they're part and parcel of the same negotiation or a later one. This is also a possibility whenever the negotiations are in the same or similar industries or areas.

The impact of setting a precedent is something the negotiator should give serious thought to during the early stages of his preparation, and frequently reconsider as the negotiation progresses. It's important for him, for example, to maintain an awareness of the direct or indirect effect one issue may have upon another, particularly little issues that may not appear to be of any significance. On occasion he may want to advance a certain position on a smaller issue, with the thought in mind of setting a favorable precedent for a later, more important issue.

The converse, of course, is also true. In fact, the numerous adverse affects that can and often do flow from setting an unfavorable precedent is a good reason why it's important for the negotiator to get in on the ground floor in most negotiations. What may appear to be an insignificant matter may later turn out to be the very bean from which the entire stalk must grow.

Setting a precedent is a common occurrence in everyday life. Give the daughter a big chocolate cake and plenty of gifts for her birthday, and she'll look for them again next year. Let the son use the family car for his big Saturday night date, and he'll ask again next week. Tip the barber a dollar, and he'll expect it next time. Even successfully talking a policeman out of a traffic ticket may merit another try with the same story unless, of course, it's the same officer.

Negotiation between a company and its union is a classic example of a situation where a precedent may be set for both the parties and the issues. The parties, of course, are the company and the union themselves as opposed to their officers or leaders, who may change from time to time. The issues are basically always the same and entail such matters as wages, fringe benefits such as medical insurance, working conditions, and others generally embodied in a written contract. As I earlier indicated, this is one of the areas where it's very important for either a smaller company or its union to get off on the right foot in their relationship. Small companies often grow into large ones, and as they grow in size, so do their unions. Hence, the early precedents that both may set can strongly influence and perhaps even govern their future relationship.

Setting a precedent may sometimes be inadvertently done in the same negotiation. To cite an experience, I was negotiating the value of several corporations. When discussing the first corporation, my opponent strongly urged that book value (net value after subtracting liabilities from assets) was an important factor to be considered. It was obviously favorable to him. I made no objection since I placed much more significance on the value of the second corporation, where book value was very unfavorable to him. When we passed on to it I took great pains to make certain that book value took the spotlight. After his great build-up as to its significance in the first, there was little he could do to play it down in the second.

Setting a precedent can often spill over into other related industries or parties in the same industries. Again, taking the company-union situation, a labor agreement with one of the steel or auto producers may cast the die for the others. Indeed, the same union is generally involved and frequently deliberately bargains on that basis, actually seeking to adopt the precedent-setting factor as part of its bargaining strategy. By selecting what it believes to be the most vulnerable producer, it not only enhances chances of a favorable agreement with that producer but also has the effects spill over onto the others.

## What to Do After a Precedent Has Been Set

The answer to this proposition depends almost entirely upon whether the precedent is favorable or unfavorable. I've indicated above how wanting to set a precedent may actually become a part of the negotiator's strategy. On other occasions it may come about unexpectedly, as in the book value situation. Whichever the case, whenever it's favorable, the negotiator should never hesitate to take full advantage of it just as I did in the book value situation. That's part and parcel of the art and skill of negotiation—to capitalize on every favorable element.

Whenever the precedent is unfavorable, it's incumbent upon the negotiator to demonstrate why it doesn't apply. Distinguishing it is perhaps the best and simplest route. Perhaps the passage of time has materially altered the circumstances. To use our company-union situation, corporate profits may have slid since the time of the precedent setting or, on the union's end, the cost of living may have sharply increased (which seems to be inevitable), thus negating past wage increases as a current, precedent-setting guide.

To take an everyday example, assume the man of the house wants to buy a new set of golf clubs from the club pro. A member of his regular foursome got a new set earlier in the year and it seems to have done wonders for his game. The club pro will undoubtedly quote him the same price his colleague had to pay. "After all," he'd probably say, "they're worth every penny. And besides, the precedent's been set. If word gets around that I'm discriminating between members, it might not go over too well."

The man of the house just happens to be a sanguine (and also shrewd) old fellow and points out to the pro that he became interested in the clubs through his friend, who praised them highly, and that he would do the same, which should bring more prospective buyers to the pro's clubhouse door (he's building up his goodwill). But more importantly, he carefully points out that it's much later in the season and discounts, whether they be publicly announced or private, are certainly good business in order to save the cost of carrying the inventory throughout the "long winter months." This approach should weaken the pro considerably and, more importantly, provide him with justification for bypassing the earlier price precedent and selling at a lower figure.

To cite another familiar illustration, assume you are a member of a civic organization that holds an awards dinner each year at the same local restaurant. The members are all pleased with the location and the food, but each year the cost seems to rise. You have been assigned the task of negotiating a lower cost. One of your greatest obstacles will obviously be past precedents—the organization has always gone along with the previous prices. But the precedent is unfavorable. You've therefore got to set out to distinguish it. Here are some ways of doing it: (1) The membership in your organization may have increased, thus increasing the restaurant owner's volume and lowering his costs; (2) Your organization may be able to make a special volume purchase from its own source of the main menu item (steaks, for example) at a lower cost, thus lowering the restaurant owner's costs; (3) A certain percentage of the membership may agree to eat at the restaurant on one or more occasions in the future to increase the restaurant owner's regular volume.

The foregoing are merely illustrative. As you can see, however, the available approaches are numerous, and all are designed to distinguish a previously set, unfavorable precedent.

# 45

# *The Importance of Maintaining Control*

I've touched upon the need for control on numerous occasions. Effective control is essential to any negotiation because it will allow the negotiator to guide the discussions toward the desired end. He will be able to follow his pre-negotiation-developed strategies and techniques, and to sustain positive momentum. But effective control is often hard to come by. It's sort of like that extra money you've been saving for a very special occasion, perhaps even a second honeymoon, when the inevitable emergency arises. Now you have it; now you don't.

### Where Effective Control Begins

Have you ever accepted the advice of others? When? Why? Did it later prove to be good or bad? In order to fully understand where effective control begins, it's necessary to ask yourself these questions. Think about them, particularly the last one. Now, let's add another. Did you ask for the advice or was it volunteered? Let me attempt to answer them and see if I'm correct.

Yes, you have accepted the advice of others. We all have. When? On numerous occasions. Why? Probably because it was available. Was it good or bad? The law of averages would, unfortunately, say bad. Now we come to the really key question. Did you ask for the advice? Again, the averages would say "No."

From the foregoing, it's apparent that effective control begins within the individual negotiator. This literally means that

174

he must exercise his own independent judgment on all matters affecting the negotiation. Accepting the advice or opinions of others, particularly if unsolicited, is one of the quickest and surest ways of losing control. By substituting or materially altering his own considered judgment for the advice or opinions of others the negotiator is, in effect, discarding all of his own preparation, training and ability—spilling it down the drain.

If he allows this practice to continue there may come a time when he may lose much of his ability to reason things out for himself, an indispensible quality that he must carry into the bargaining. When this occurs, failure will be staring him directly in the face. Drastic? Certainly! It's for that reason that I always follow this simple rule: Never place yourself in the position of allowing others to venture out with *unsolicited* advice. I emphasize the word unsolicited because none of us are infallible. If the advice of others is needed, never hesitate to ask. You may want to consider it in arriving at your decision—but always be certain that it is truly your decision. This may appear unduly harsh on those who are kind enough to offer the advice, but it's really for their best interests and certainly yours. Neither you nor they will have to suffer the consequences of any faulty advice. And each time you set your own course, you're actually taking an important step toward maintaining effective control.

## Additional Practices to Insure Effective Control

There are numerous practices that the negotiator can put into effect in order to help insure control. I've already mentioned various means throughout the text, such as the use of leading questions. Here are some additional important ways:

—All announcements affecting the negotiation should come from either the negotiator or from a designated source. On important matters, particularly thos‿ that involve newsworthy items, it is generally sheer disaster to violate this rule. Unwanted publicity and the resulting public reaction can easily polarize the parties' positions even though they may want to remain flexible. For this reason the better practice is to restrict all remarks to a terse "no comment" or "a full text of the details will be released as soon as an agreement has been reached."

On occasion, a negotiator may want to release information as a matter of strategy in order to increase his leverage and thus apply pressure to the other side. Never lose sight of the fact, however, that this approach is a two-edged sword that can cut you as deeply as your opponent if not skillfully handled.

—Be certain that all files or other written data pertinant to the negotiation are kept secure. This may seem like a relatively unimportant matter, but let me draw from an experience to show you what can happen.

During the course of negotiating a multi-issue matter, my opponent refused to budge on the value of a comparatively minor issue, even though he was unable to provide any real justification for his position. By skillfully probing, I was able to learn that sometime before I had assumed responsibility for the negotiation (others had previously been involved) he had come upon several personal letters indicating in very general terms that the asset had some value. The letters swayed him to such a great extent that he was unable to objectively examine existing facts in order to arrive at a value.

—All memoranda written to others should be appropriately labeled as "confidential" so that the recipients are made fully aware of their true nature. From the experience cited above it is clear that written data can go astray. Appropriately labeling them, therefore, can add some degree of assurance of security and thus facilitate control.

—Last but not least, it goes without saying that the negotiator should be "tight-lipped" about all matters that may touch upon the negotiation. Disclosures should be restricted to only those authorized to receive them.

## An Everyday Example of How to Maintain Effective Control

Assume you and your neighbor have been having a dispute over the boundary line of your adjoining properties. No survey has ever been taken on the property line and frequent discussions between you and him have not yet resolved the matter. You are confident, however, that progress has been made and an eventual favorable settlement will be reached. To assist in maintaining effective control, every family member with knowledge of the matter should be instructed not to discuss it with others, *including* the neighbor with whom you're having the dispute. This will not only prevent unwarranted rumors from floating about and perhaps getting back to your neighbor, but also allow you to retain complete control over what's happening and, more importantly, what's about to happen. If the discussions are in a friendly state and you want to consult an engineer to make a survey or a lawyer to review the legal description of the property contained in your deed, let your neighbor know· what you are going to do. The reason, of course, is not to get his permission, since you are free to do as you wish, but to keep him advised so that he doesn't learn of it secondhand and perhaps misconstrue your intentions.

Your lawyer is duty-bound to maintain the matter in strict confidence. You should instruct the engineer to do likewise. As you can see, what you are doing is allowing yourself to guide the discussions toward the desired end without allowing outside influences to intervene. This will better enable you to follow your strategies and techniques and to sustain positive negotiation momentum, the two essential reasons for maintaining control.

# 46

# *Avoiding Predictability*

Many things in life are predictable with absolute certainty. We know, for example, that fire will burn, water will drench, snow is cold, and death and taxes are unavoidable. Others, although perhaps not completely predictable, are more than likely to occur. We can normally assume that the other driver will stop at the stop sign; that the products on the grocery shelf are reasonably fresh; and that when the telephone rings, someone will be on the other end. Still others are obviously impossible to predict. Will the stock market be bullish or bearish next year? Will it rain next month?

If someone would invite you to play golf, you would normally expect to tee off on the first hole and play straight through to hole number eighteen. Your system becomes gauged to the course, and as you approach each hole, your strategy is formulated on that basis, particularly if you have played on the course before. The third hole is a par four. A strong drive and a good wedge should be good enough to get on the green and put you in shape for a shot at a birdie. From there, a well-placed two iron on the hilly fourth hole should again put you in contention for a birdie. The entire course is more or less mentally preplanned in this manner with the hope, of course, that lady luck will provide an additional boost. But what if you played the first and second holes and suddenly your opponent suggested that you play the eighth, ninth, and seventeenth holes, and then go back to the third? Would it break your stride and perhaps even leave your game in a shambles, like a pile of new-mown hay?

A negotiator's moves should never be predictable with any certainty. If they are, he will be giving his opponent a very decided edge, since it may allow him to preplan his moves to counter those of the negotiator. In addition, it will deprive the negotiator of the freshness that's a prerequisite to successful negotiation.

When I was a young negotiator first learning the psychology of negotiation, I noticed that the moves of many of my opponents could be easily anticipated. At first this troubled me because I felt that if their's could, perhaps so could mine. I soon came to realize, however, that predictability was like any other negotiation pitfall. It could be overcome, but only with thorough knowledge of its existance and *conscious* mental effort.

I place strong emphasis on the word "conscious" because there are many ways to unknowingly fall into its unsuspecting trap. Some are so subtle that they may actually sneak up on the negotiator, as April 15 sometimes does on a taxpayer. For example, I negotiated a matter where a party to the negotiation prepared a very detailed spread sheet, showing at different percentages the ultimate dollar figures that would be payable in the event of a settlement at any of these percentages. The percentages, of course, were arbitrarily arrived at. Whenever settlement possibilities were discussed, reference was made to the spread sheet as though it were a map to the fabled Blackbeard's treasure. The more the sheet was referred to the more the party's thinking centered around it, until eventually almost everything that he suggested originated from it in one form or another. He was, of course, unknowingly making his moves predictable.

On other occasions, falling into the trap of predictability can be more obvious. Consistently coming in with high demands is a common example. Labor negotiators frequently fall into this trap. The union often comes in with very high claims and the company with very low ones. This frequently results in a strike which, of course, benefits no one.

Recently, I happened to engage in a friendly discussion with a member of management of a large company that was involved in labor negotiations. He indicated that things were not going too well and that the relationship between the company and the union heads seemed to be at a standstill. He also related that some of the union rank and file were entitled to some benefits which the company had the right to, and had decided to terminate in view of the current labor problems. I suggested to the fellow that perhaps the company should have considered doing precisely the opposite, namely, allowing the benefits in full.

"Why?" he asked perplexedly.

"Because," I replied, "the company was doing exactly what the union had probably expected. If the company would have allowed the benefits and said to the rank and file, 'Look, we're going to give you these benefits because we want you to know that we are not unreasonable and want to develop and maintain good relationships,' the move would have undoubtedly caught them off guard and certainly created a favorable impression, particularly on those entitled to the benefits. It may have also helped in creating the type of reasonable environment that is so necessary to successful negotiation."

## Where the Danger of Predictability is Greatest

There are two situations where the danger of predictability is greatest. The first is cases which are similar to those previously handled by the negotiator.

Lawyers are sometimes prone to fall into set patterns because of frequent exposure to repetitious situations. Characterizing an automobile case as a "rear-ender" or "intersection accident," or a federal estate tax case as a "Section 2036," for example, tends to set off a whole chain of pre-developed mental reactions, and thus cement their thinking on the strategies and techniques to be employed. Of course, in most instances certain procedures have been set up which are fairly mechanical and must be followed—filing dates and motions are examples. But the vast areas in between leave ample room for fresh, imaginative thinking, and it is in these areas that predictability should never be present.

The second area is where negotiations are frequently carried on between the same persons, even though the issues or matters to be negotiated are different. This is fairly common and arises, for instance, in personal injury cases handled by the same claim adjuster, tax cases when the same agent is involved, labor negotiations, and many, many others. Often the parties may get to know each other so well that they automatically adopt the same moves, so that one can predict with great certainty what the other will do.

## How To Avoid Predictability

The simplest and most effective way to avoid predictability is to take a fresh and imaginative look at *every* negotiation. This includes all of the issues, the opponent or opponents, and every other aspect. The negotiator should frequently ask himself whether his approach is based upon an objective analysis of the merits, or whether he's doing it that way merely because that's the way he normally handles such cases. Often he will find that his thinking has become solidified and his approach entirely anticipated. Some danger signals to be on the alert for are lack of enthusiasm or a feeling of comfortableness during the course of preparation. If the adrenalin has completely ceased flowing, the challenge may have settled down to a comfortable feeling of doing something the way it's always been done. Certainly, as the negotiator develops experience, many matters will flow smoothly. Nevertheless, it's important for him to realize that his strategy and techniques must be freshly thought out. Otherwise, he may be greatly decreasing his own chances of success.

Another good way is for the negotiator to drop clichés and other set catch-phrases or labels from his vocabulary. As I've already indicated, they tend to mentally bind him in. Terms such as those previously mentioned, namely, "rear-ender," "intersection accident" and "Section 2036" should be eliminated, as should numerous others, such as "wheeler-dealer" if you are involved in the real estate area, "tight-fisted," "conservative" or "dour" if in the banking area, and even "housewife" if dealing with the lady of the house. (You may ask why the latter. By characterizing the lady of the house as a "housewife" you are, in effect, mentally placing her in a mold that she may or may not fit. It is far better to drop the term from your thinking and approach her on a completely fresh and objective basis.)

Note that the techniques set forth in this text are not in any particular order and may not all be used in every negotiation. On the contrary, they are tools designed to facilitate the construction of a successful negotiation. Just as a carpenter needs only saw and hammer to cut and nail a board, often only a few techniques may be necessary when the matter to be negotiated is fairly simple and routine. But just as all of the tools in the tool box must eventually be used before an entire house has been constructed, most, if not all, of the techniques may come into play in some negotiations. This involves the individual judgment of the negotiator. Whichever the case, he should never play his holes in order, from one through eighteen. It is far better that he plays them as he sees them. If he maintains that type of flexibility, it will be virtually impossible for his opponent to predict his moves and to formulate his strategy and techniques based upon what he anticipates the negotiator will do.

# 47

# When to Intentionally Break Off Negotiations

There are two situations when it is advisable to intentionally break off negotiations. The first is when progress has reached an apparent standstill and another avenue for negotiating the matter exists. This is always true, for example, in the federal tax area. In the event of non-agreement with the agent, other opportunities are available at higher levels, such as the Appellate level. If the negotiator is of the opinion that he will receive much more favorable treatment at a higher level, he should not hesitate to break off the discussions. This will provide him with an opportunity to sit down with "new" opponents, who may react more favorably to the issues involved and the negotiator's approach to them.

A similar situation may prevail in numerous other instances. When dealing with large corporations or financial institutions such as banks or trust companies, there is invariably a "higher source of appeal" which can be tapped in the event the negotiator feels that he can make better progress. Underlings often take unreasonable positions on relatively small or unimportant issues. Their motives vary—some may be the weak type, reluctant to make decisions, while others may be new on the job and uncertain as to the precise nature and extent of their authority. Or they may be so close to the matter that, as the old saying goes, they are "unable to see the forest for the trees." In any event, the negotiator should not hesitate to break off the discussions whenever he feels that a better, more progressive avenue exists.

A second situation is when an opponent is merely attempting to "go to school." Occasionally there is really no sincere effort on an opponent's part to reach a favorable agreement. Indeed, he may have not been sincere at the outset, or he may have closed his mind to any agreement and is attempting to reap side benefits from continuing the discussions.

This situation occurs most often when the opponent is the one who has instituted the negotiations. Perhaps he may express an interest in purchasing an asset owned or controlled by the negotiator or his client. His real intent, however, may be to acquire information or knowledge not otherwise available to him. Hence the phrase "going to school." It's always important for the negotiator to remain alert to this possibility. Whenever he determines its presence, he should immediately break off the discussions.

### Ways To Detect When an Opponent May Be "Going to School"

Since the negotiator is dealing with the state of mind of his opponent, situations where his opponent lacks sincerity may often be very difficult to detect. Here, however, are several important clues to its presence.

First, if his opponent has requested data or information that is clearly outside the scope of the matter to be negotiated, and is unable to reasonably justify the reason for the request, it is axiomatic that his motives must be something other than what he has indicated.

Second, if his proposals are unusual or even outlandish, there's another strong indication that he lacks sincerity and has other motives. Care should be taken here. Sometimes an unreasonable or outlandish proposal is made through ignorance or simple lack of information or familiarity. If he's offering a price equal to only one-third of what the negotiator can get for the asset elsewhere, he may be unfamiliar with its true character, particularly if it is real estate, which varies widely from location to location. On the other hand, he may simply be after information about the property not otherwise available.

An area where "going to school" is fairly common is, again, in the Federal tax area. Often an agent has already made up his mind not to go along with a taxpayer's proposal, but fails to disclose his intentions until he has requested and received all of the supporting data that he can get. He may be reluctant to go along because the issue is too large and he therefore doesn't want to take the responsibility, or simply because his immediate supervisor has already "dictated" what his position should be. Whatever the case, seldom will the agent disclose his non-acquiescent attitude until after he's received the desired information or supporting data.

This operates to considerably strengthen both the government's hand and the agent's. The government is provided with an opportunity to carefully consider it when formulating its strategy. In addition, some degree of emphasis is added to the agent's determination (which he must substantiate in his written report) since he can maintain he arrived at it after considering all of the data, even though his mind had been foreclosed early. Hence, whenever the negotiator senses this situation, it is far better to break off the discussions and make a full disclosure at a higher level in order to increase his chances of receiving a more objective and favorable look at the matter.

"Going to school" situations are fairly common when corporations are involved, particularly among competitors. The opponent's reasoning looks something like this: "I'll make a merger pitch and ask for certain data. If I get it, I'll consider it. If it looks good, I'll pursue it. If not, I'm still ahead, since I've had a look at information not otherwise available." The negotiator should take care, therefore, to be certain of the sincerity of his opponent. In most instances, the majority will be completely sincere. On other occasions, some will not. Always be alert to this latter possibility.

# 48
# Jest and Earnestness

*"You think this market is tough, in our old neighborhood the canaries sang bass."*

—Overheard in a stockbroker's office during the depths of a bear market.

Occasionally the negotiation atmosphere may become extremely tense, as though a time bomb were about to explode. It may come about because of such factors as the touchiness of the subject matter involved, unwise or untimely utterances by one or more of the negotiating parties, past misunderstandings not directly associated with the negotiations, or even from pressures wholly outside the discussions, such as unwarranted publicity. When this occurs, one of the best means of bringing the situation back to a state of normality is through the tactful and tasteful use of humor. " ... humor, more than anything else in the human make-up, can afford an aloofness and an ability to rise above any situation, even if only for a few seconds."[5]

A good approach to interjecting humor into the discussions is by poking fun at one's self. Abraham Lincoln was a master at this, often turning around an otherwise tense and very serious situation with a jest about his scraggly appearance or manner of speech. Certainly all of us at one time or another have done or said something outlandish enough to provide both ourselves and others

---

[5]Victor E. Frankl, MAN'S SEARCH FOR MEANING (New York: Washington Square Press, Inc. 1967). p. 68.

with a good laugh. I can recall such an incident during my college days. I was giving a speech before the class on what I considered to be the finer points of the game of golf. Instead of using a two iron on an imaginary two hundred and twenty-five yard hole, I inadvertently used a "two-hundred and twenty-five yard two iron." It got an excellent laugh from the class, but unfortunately I didn't discover the error until after I had finished. Otherwise, I would have joined in.

I am not necessarily restricting humor in this discussion to outright laughter, but rather to include anything that has a tendency to alleviate an otherwise tense situation. A self-depreciating statement, for example, may actually add a sufficient air of lightness and thus come within the definition of humor.

To illustrate, Benjamin Franklin used this technique when arguing for the adoption of the United States Constitution. By questioning his own wisdom some say that his words, coming in the closing hours of the convention, were largely responsible for final adoption. They are worthy of quoting here in order to illustrate how he successfully employed this technique:

> I confess that there are several parts of this Constitution which I do not at present approve; but I am not sure I shall never approve them. For, having lived long, I have experienced many instances of being obliged, by better information, or fuller consideration, to change opinions even on important subjects, which I once thought right, but found to be otherwise. It is, therefore, that the older I grow, the more apt I am to doubt my own judgment, and to pay more respect to the judgment of others. . . . Thus, I consent, Sir, to this Constitution because I expect no better, and because I am not sure that it is not the best. . . . On the whole, Sir, I cannot help expressing a wish that every member of the Convention who may still have objections to it, would, with me, on this occasion doubt a little of his own infallibility, and to make manifest our unanimity, put his name to this instrument.

Finally, a word of caution. The humor sought to be interjected into the negotiation should be relevant to either the parties or the subject matter. Otherwise it may appear awkward and out of place, and thus only serve to compound the tenseness or even be construed as an insult. Poking fun at one's self with self-depreciating statements generally satisfies this requirement since the negotiator is, of course, personally involved in and an integral part of the discussions. If he can also tie the humor in with the subject matter, it will have even greater impact. This may often be done through similarities. If, for instance, you're negotiating a real estate matter, a bit of humor about an incident involving another real estate matter should suffice to adequately tie the two together.

Just as humor may normalize a tense and serious situation, interjecting earnestness into a humorous situation can have a similar effect. Sometimes an opponent may consider a particular matter trivial and thus treat it with jest, while the negotiator may consider it to be a serious matter or perhaps may want to lead into another subject of a more serious nature, but before doing so wants to subside any lightness.

To illustrate, assume you're negotiating the settlement of a personal injury case. Your client, an attractive young lady, slipped on a wet floor in a crowded department store and landed in a very embarrassing position, in addition to suffering serious injuries. Describing the fall may tend to put your opponent in a humorous state of mind or perhaps even provoke laughter, particularly if he has thoroughly investigated the matter and taken statements from witnesses. Your description may be refreshing his recollection of these earlier accounts. Immediately following with specifics of the serious nature of the injuries or merely calling them tactfully to his attention, however, should bring the matter quickly back to a more serious vane. This is a technique often employed by skillful trial attorneys to invoke sympathy for their clients from the jury, when opposing counsel is attempting to make a jest in order to minimize the injuries and thus any compensation for them.

One last thought: people are more apt to respond to specific situations as opposed to generalities. If someone were to tell us of the poverty that exists in certain parts of the world, it would undoubtedly concern us as human beings. The impact would be greater, however, if one individual case were described, perhaps with some photographs of the impoverished person. It's important, therefore, for the negotiator to deal in specifics whenever attempting to use earnestness to combat jest.

# *49*

# *Closing the Negotiation*

*"You have taken ship, you have made the voyage,
you have come to port; disembark."*
Marcus Aurelius

Nothing is more vital than knowing when and how to close the negotiation. A negotiator who is unable to successfully master the ability to close is a "talker," nothing more. It's the close that the entire negotiation centers around, the negotiator's ultimate destination. Here are some essential elements of closing, together with some important "do's and don'ts" and closing techniques.

**When to Close**

No two negotiations are alike. Opponents and issues may and usually do differ, as well as numerous other aspects of a negotiation. There is therefore no set moment to close or, for that matter, length of time to negotiate. Rather, it depends almost entirely upon at what point an opponent will be most likely to say "Yes."

It's up to the negotiator to determine when the negotiation has reached that stage. Here's where continuous experience, a keen sense of judgment, and an in-depth knowledge of people pay off. Great care is required—care not to attempt to close prematurely or too late. Sometimes it may be wiser to continue discussions at another session rather than attempt to close at an earlier one. On

189

other occasions, dragging the discussions beyond a point when they could have been earlier closed may be equally as disastrous. In any event, the essential point is for the negotiator to continuously strive to develop a keen sense of judgment as to when his opponent will most likely say "Yes."

## Some Important DO'S and DON'TS

*DO:*

1. Once an issue or the entire negotiation is closed, be certain it remains closed. For example, I was negotiating during lunch with several opponents. The matter was successfully concluded, and I shook hands right on the spot even though we were all going to ride back to the office together. During the ride over the conversation was strictly non-business. By dwelling on matters already settled, I would have been needlessly running the risk of reopening them.

2. Whenever closing a discussion where some points are agreed upon and others remain open for later discussion, always try to summarize those that are agreed upon in order to avoid any later misunderstandings and to help insure their finality. This will also tend to leave an opponent in a "Yes" attitude which is conducive to later negotiation progress.

3. It's generally better to close right at the negotiating session. "Thinking it over" or other forms of procrastination frequently lead to non-agreement. The negotiator should be fully prepared to close *before* any session. This means that if he can get his opponent to agree by demonstrating the soundness of his position, he should, whenever he feels the time is ripe, move to close. I once sat in on a negotiation where the negotiator did a very beautiful job of demonstrating his position. When it came time to close, however, he said, "Don't make up your mind now. Think it over." He was never able to fully recover. In short, he became a talker.

An important exception to this "DO" is when newly discovered facts enter into the picture, usually during the course of the discussions. Frequently, the negotiator may want to fully analyze them before taking any action. He's thus not really ready to close and shouldn't attempt to do so until he has had ample opportunity to examine the new data.

*DON'T:*

1. Never overclose! Once you've reached a point when you feel the matter is settled—STOP! Continuing can only complicate matters and you may find that what was once an agreed-upon item is again unagreed. Experience will tell you when you've reached the "point of no return."

2. Never completely annihilate an opponent. Always leave him with something to feel good about. Otherwise, you may have made yourself an enemy. I always try to negotiate a matter as though I will again have the occasion and opportunity to deal with my opponent. Your opponents will learn to respect you on the basis of your ability and most are wise enough to realize that you have a job to do, as do they. So leave them something to feel good about.

## Closing Techniques

There are numerous so-called "closing techniques." Below are listed several of the most useful. It's important for the negotiator to fully realize, however, that their application should be restricted to acting as a cue for the close and *not* as a device for actually "winning" any negotiation. On the contrary, if the negotiator hasn't amply demonstrated the soundness of his position prior to employing a closing technique, it will afford him little, if any, value, and can actually work to his detriment. No opponent likes to feel he's being strong-armed into an agreement.

*PROMPTING ACTION TECHNIQUE*

This technique may be particularly useful when the negotiator feels confident that the time has come to close. He prompts the close by calling upon his opponent to take some form of action, usually in the form of an affirmative act or response. "Please sign here" or "Don't you agree" are two examples.

*ASSUMPTION TECHNIQUE*

This technique differs from the previous technique in that here the negotiator actually assumes his opponent will agree and thus institutes the closing action. "I'll call the bank and ask them

to set up the escrow" is an example, or the negotiator may simply
sign a document and hand it to the opponent for signature.

## SUMMARIZING TECHNIQUE

Here the negotiator summarizes with a terse statement of the
parties' understanding. Closing in this manner has the additional
advantage of making a much greater impact and thus making it
much more unlikely that an opponent will resist. Moreover, if he is
in disagreement with any of the points raised, it will afford him a
final opportunity to say so. It's important for the negotiator,
therefore, to be certain that there is no disagreement at this point,
so that the effect of the technique is to close and not to rekindle
or raise new arguments. Greater skill is thus required with this
technique.

Here's an everyday example of how this technique might
work. Assume three of your favorite, very large elm trees con-
tracted Dutch Elm disease and died. You find that cutting them
down and removing the stumps is an expensive proposition. In
addition, you would like to have them removed fairly soon in
order to have some fruit trees planted, and to comply with a city
ordinance requiring early removal in order to prevent spread of the
disease. You have talked with several tree removal people, and one
in particular quotes you a price and a time removal period that is
attractive. You therefore want to close right away, before any
complications set in. Notice that the negotiator's summation is
framed with positive sentences rather than with questions. The
idea is to close the negotiation, not to leave your opponent with
an opening to re-negotiate.

Negotiator: "You will cut down all three trees, haul all of the
wood away, remove the stumps, and fill the holes suitably for
resodding. The job is to be completed by the twenty-first of this
month. It's going to cost me four hundred and fifty dollars—two
hundred payable when work begins and the balance due upon
completion of the work to my satisfaction."

Opponent: "Right."

# 50

# *Experience vs. Repetition*

Books are good sources from which to accumulate knowledge, but knowledge without practical application is virtually useless. It is application that separates the spectator from the participant.

The same, of course, is true in negotiation. For the person who sincerely desires to become an expert at the art and skill of negotiation, one of his first and continuous steps is reading. That's the primary reason why I've taken the time and effort to write this text and to disclose principles and techniques that have taken me many years to perfect—to provide the reader with a source from which to form a solid basis for learning the art and skill of negotiation.

A second essential step is for a person to place himself on the firing line in as many *diverse* negotiation situations as humanly possible. I emphasize the word "diverse" because too often one is apt to confuse repetition with experience. What is referred to as ten years of experience is in reality often only one or two years of experience with eight or nine years of repetition.

Experience will condition one's thinking to the different situations that he encounters. It will teach him to remain cool and confident under the tremendous pressures that are frequently associated with negotiation. It'll help him to leave his emotions inside where they belong. And it will even act as a beacon to warn him of the many dangerous rocks and shallows that he must successfully navigate along the way toward a successful conclusion to most negotiations.

Repetition, nevertheless, has its usefulness, too. It's repetition that will save the negotiator time in preparation and research. He's driven down the lane before and knows where each stop and sharp turn will be as well as at what point the ferocious canine will leap out to challenge him as he glides by.

Since both experience and repetition, then, are so important to the art and skill of negotiation, the essential inquiry becomes: What constitutes experience and what repetition? Or, to put it another way, when does experience cease to be experience and become repetition?

Someone recently asked me if I'd read a particular article on the terrible thing a young person had done while under the influence of narcotics.

"No," I replied. Some time earlier I'd already read of a similar incident that, unfortunately, would have been hard to surpass. Anything after that would have been merely repetitious as to the adverse effects of narcotics on a young mind.

If a real estate man has negotiated the sale of twenty homes, can it be said that he is now an experienced salesman? What if all of the homes were in one well-situated development with only a few different home designs, and all fairly priced in the same range and thus appealing to a limited segment of the market? He's probably very short on experience and long on repetition. What if, however, every home were of a different locale, age, price, and for a different market? The converse would be true. Indeed, he may be longer on experience than a colleague who has already sold two hundred or more homes!

The answer to the question, then, runs back to the key word "diverse." The negotiator should strive to gain as many varied negotiating experiences as humanly possible. Each will add to his store of knowledge, and as his shelves fill, he will see that with the additional, important ingredient of mastering the psychology of successful negotiation he will soon become more successful every time he sits down to negotiate.

# 51

# Broadening the Negotiator's Educational Base

It's important for the negotiator to constantly strive to broaden the base of his knowledge in order to be more effective at the bargaining table. Haphazard excursions into a multiplicity of available data is not to be recommended. On the contrary, the negotiator should here again be highly selective as to what he takes into his "brain-attic" in order not to let "useless" information "elbow out the useful."

Listed below, in the order of what I consider their importance from the standpoint of contribution to the negotiator's continued education, are four areas of study which should assist him as he goes about his daily activities of attempting to demonstrate to others the soundness of his positions.

The most essential area is works which will assist in understanding human nature. It takes a minimum of two to negotiate. Thus, knowledge of human nature is essential. To be sure, the best way to acquire it is by actual contact with others. Books, however, can provide an important supplement if properly selected. Those that I recommend are by the masters, such as Plato, Aristotle, Marcus Aurelius, Cicero, and Freud.

A second important area in which the negotiator should continue to increase his knowledge is any technical area that he has the occasion to primarily or frequently negotiate in. A sound personal injury trial lawyer, for example, should be as well versed in medical terms as most practicing physicians. Similarly, a skilled union negotiator should make every effort to master such matters as balance sheets and accounting terms and principles, in order to become more effective at the bargaining table when he sits down with company representatives.

There are so many independent areas of specialization that I will not endeavor to list any specific works. Suffice it to say that the negotiator should never hesitate to make every available effort to find good sources within his specialty in order to enhance his knowledge and thus his chances of success.

Another essential area helpful to almost any negotiator is the general trend of the times. What's the economic outlook of a particular industry, or even the entire country? Will business profits be up? Has anything new been happening that may affect his particular area? These are just a few of the areas in which a skilled negotiator should be knowledgeable. I once asked a contact lens specialist about a new lens that had been developed in Germany which I had then recently read about. He didn't know it existed. Do you think it might have made him a more effective specialist if he were completely up to date on every single development in his field? The same rule applies to negotiation!

Weekly news magazines and trade journals are a good source of what's happening around the country and, indeed, the world. Local newspapers, too, may be helpful, but take care here since they may be slanted to favor one position or another, and it therefore may not be possible to get a truly objective picture.

Finally, seminars and other similar gatherings are a good source of new information. I place these last on my list because attending them can often be very time consuming. Care and skill in selection are therefore very important. Nevertheless, if they are done well they can be very useful.

One of the first litigation matters that I became involved in as a lawyer was favorably advanced by my attendance at a local bar association meeting. I represented the plaintiff. The defendant, prior to my entering the case, had taken a sworn statement from my client which he refused to produce. The then-existing law supported his refusal. At the bar session, the speaker commented on a recent but yet unreported decision which reversed the law in this area. By merely calling my opponent and advising him of the opinion, I was able to get the statement without the necessity of further legal maneuvers.

If the negotiator can get one helpful idea or thought from a seminar, he should consider it a success. Two or more and he's got a real bonus! For lawyers, many bar associations and law schools have outstanding programs. Programs that I generally find very good and therefore recommend are those given by the Practicing Law Institute. For non-professional negotiators, there are many miscellaneous seminars of interest. Be selective. Try to attend only those that appear most likely to give results.

# 52

# *Prayer*

*"Wisdom is the principal thing; therefore
get wisdom:"*
PROVERBS 4:7

I never begin a negotiation, large or small, without prayer. Seldom, if ever, do I pray for success, but for wisdom and courage. Wisdom to understand both the problems and my opponent and to exercise good judgment in all of my decisions, large or small. Courage to stand by my convictions even though the stakes may be high and others more willing to compromise than push forward.

Conrad Hilton called faith the only "gilt-edged security." It was the rock-like foundation on which he stood and was guided to world prominence in the competitive hotel field. I think perhaps it's even more than that. Certainly faith has been the backbone of every one of my negotiations. It has guided me successfully through some of the most difficult and complex ones imaginable.

# *Index*

## A

"A Study in Scarlet," 40n
Ability, mental, of negotiator as
    main weapon, 19
Accuracy essential in correspondence, 80
Advice of others, danger in constantly
    following, 174-177
Agreement as ultimate objective of
    negotiating, 128
Allen, Ethan, 86
"Alternate approach" system of reducing
    anxiety, 117
Anger in negotiation, place of, 102-106
    basics of, 102-103
        as negative emotion, 102
    "controlled" anger, learning to use,
        106
    negotiation, influence upon,
        103-105
    opponent's, what to do with, 105
    question of, 105-106
*Annotated Sherlock Holmes,* 40n
Announcements concerning negotiation,
    policy concerning, 175
Answers, obvious, questions calling for,
    143-144
Anxiety, effect of upon negotiation,
    113-117
    "alternate approach" system, 117
    example of effectiveness of,
        113-114
    reducing or eliminating, 116-117
    as state of mind, 114
    using effectively, 114-115

Appearance of negotiator, physical,
    35-38
    clothes, 35-37
        neckties, 36-37
    mannerisms, 37-38
        eye contact, 37-38
        gestures, 37-38
        object, using to emphasize
           point, 38
Appearance of opponent sometimes
    deceiving, 94
Arguments, potentially troublesome,
    disposing of, 158-160
    key words, use of, 158-159
Aristotle, 149, 195
Art and skill in negotiations,
    meaning of, 17-20
    merits of position, determining,
        18-19
    qualities necessary, 19
    pressures of negotiations, how to
        hold up under, 19-20
    bridge of trust, creating, 20,
        161-163
    understanding of self, 20
Assistants, selection and use of, 62-64
Association, 51
Assumption technique of closing,
    191-192
Attitude of negotiator, mental, 33-34
    developing, 33-34
Authority for negotiating, final, 89-93
    how to determine, 90-91
    joint authority, 92-93
    strategy, 91-92

# B

Bad habits, common, avoiding, 73-75
Baring-Gould, William S., 40n
Bases, negotiating, importance of maintaining, 68-72
  primary, 68-70
  secondary, 70-72
"Beam balance" of equalization, 107-108
Beginning of negotiation, 82-84
  on friendly note, 83
Belief in self, complete, essential for negotiating success, 33
Blinking, learning to avoid, 73
Breaking off negotiations, intentional, 183-185
  in federal tax area, 183
  "going to school," opponent's, 184
    ways to detect, 184-185
Bridge of trust, building, 161-163
  (see also "Goodwill, building")
    importance of, 20

# C

Choice, use of questions, requiring, 144-145
Churchill, Sir Winston, 129, 129n
Cicero, 195
Clarification of position through correspondence, 79
Clear speaking, practicing, 76
"Client," meaning of, 7
  presence of, 25-29
    "two tier" conference, 28
Closing negotiation, 189-192
  "do's" and "don'ts," list of, 190-191
  techniques, 191-192
    assumption, 191-192
    prompting action, 191
    summarizing, 192
  when, 189-190
Clothes, importance of, 35-37
  neckties, 36-37
Comfortableness in preparation as danger signal of predictability, 181
Commencement of negotiation, 82-84
  on friendly note, 83

Concentration, 49
Confidence essential quality for negotiator, 19
Consistency important in negotiating, 19
Control, maintaining, importance of, 174-177
  example of, 176-177
  practices, additional, to insure, 175-176
  where it begins, 174-175
Control device, correspondence as, 77-78
"Controlled" anger, learning to use, 106
Coolness essential for negotiator, 105-106
Correspondence in negotiation, use of, 77-81
  accuracy, 80
  to clarify or restate positions, 79
  for deemphasis, 78
  as effective control device, 77-78
  neatness, 80
  postage, using proper, 80
  promptness, 80-81
  stationery, importance of, 80
  who should receive, 79-80
Counter-offer, making, 167-169
  definition, 167
  guidelines, essential, 167-168
    flexibility, importance of, 168
  initial offer, who makes, 168-169
  strategies, types of, 169
Courage as indispensable quality, 19

# D

Darrow, Clarence, 60
Decisions, importance of making your own, 174-177
Deemphasis, use of correspondence for, 78
Definiteness of words' meanings, importance of, 54-55
Demonstrative exhibits, use of, 164-166
  visibility of, constant, 165-166
Descriptive questions, use of, 142
Descriptive words, using, 53-54
Disclosures concerning negotiations, keeping to minimum, 176
Diversification, 50-51
Diversity in negotiating situations essential, 193-194

"Do's" and "don'ts" of closing
    negotiations, 190-191
Doyle, Sir Arthur Conan, 40n

# E

Earnestness, jests and, 186-188
    relevance of humor vital, 187-188
    specifics, use of, 188
Educational base of negotiator,
        broadening, 195-197
    human nature, knowledge of
        essential, 195
    through seminars and similar
        gatherings, 196-197
    in technical area most often
        encountered, 195-196
    trend of times, general, 196
Emotion, negative, anger as, 102
Emotional appeal, 149-154
    dominance of, 150
    through recognition, 151-153
    through self-preservation, 153-154
    through wealth, 150-151
        value as disproportionate, 151
Emotions, allowing dominance of as
        sure way to stifle negotiating
        progress, 101
Enthusiasm essential for negotiator, 19
    lack of as danger signal of
        predictability, 181
Environment, physical, 30-32
    interruptions, avoiding, 30
    neatness, importance of, 31
Equalization, necessity for, 107-110
    attaining, 108-110
    conclusion, 110
    what it is, 107-108
        "beam balance," 107-108
Exhibits, demonstrative, use of,
        164-166
    visibility of, constant, 165-166
Experience vs. repetition, 193-194
    diverse situations, importance of,
        193-194
    reading as first step, 193
Extrapolation, art of, 139-140
    definition of, 139
Eye contact, direct, importance of, 37-38
    with opponent, practicing, 75-76

# F

Facial features, observing, 123-124
Faith as "gilt-edged security," 198
Favor for opponent, benefit of doing,
        161-163 (see also "Goodwill,
        building")
Fidgeting, constant, as bad habit, 74-75
Final negotiating authority, determin-
        ing, 89-93
    how, 90-91
    joint authority, 92-93
    strategy, 91-92
Flexibility essential for negotiation, 19
Flowing through, art of, 147-148
Foerster, Friedrick, 123
Folder method of systematizing issues,
        59
Frankl, Victor E., 186n
Franklin, Benjamin, 187
Freud, 195
Friendly beginning of negotiation
        essential, 83
Fundamental areas of issue, working
        to define, 40-41

# G

General questions, 141
Gestures, use of, 37
"Gilt-edged security," faith as, 198
"Going to school" by opponent as
        reason for breaking off negotia-
        tions, 184
    ways to detect, 184-185
Golden Rule of negotiation, 97
Good habits, developing, 75-76
Goodwill, building, 161-163
    how to build, 162-163
    what it is, 161
    why necessary, 162

# H

Habit, 73-76
    bad, avoiding common, 73-75
    good, developing, 75-76
Harriman, E.H., 33
Harrow School, 129n

Hilton, Conrad, 198
Human nature, knowledge of essential,
    195
Humor, value of, 186-188
    relevance vital, 187-188

# I

"I" and "me" as part of "self," 99
Inks, use of different colors of to
    organize materials, 59
Interrupting opponent as bad habit,
    73-74
Interruptions, avoiding, 30
Inversion, avoiding danger of, 111-112
    definition, 111

# J

James, William 98
Jest and earnestness, 186-188
    relevance of humor vital, 187-188
    specifics, use of, 188
Joint negotiating authority, 92-93

# L

Language, new, introducing into
    negotiations, 137
Language of negotiator, 52-55
    definiteness of meaning, 54-55
    descriptive, 53-54
    naturalness, 53
    simple, need for, 52-53
    technical words, becoming
        acquainted with, 54
Language of opponent, concentrating
    on to gain offensive, 87
Lateral vision, using to observe,
    124-125
Leading questions, 142-143
Least resistance, following path of,
    147-148
Letter, threatening, how to handle
    receipt of, 77-78
Lincoln, Abraham, 56, 186

# M

Man's Search for Meaning, 186n
Mannerisms of negotiator, 37-38

eye contact, 37-38
gestures, 37
object, using to emphasize point, 38
Marcus Aurelius, 134, 189, 195
"Me" and "I" as part of "self," 99
Memory, negotiating, how to develop,
    49-51
    association, 51
    concentration, 49
    diversification, 50-51
Mental ability main weapon of
    negotiator, 19
Mental attitude of negotiator, 33-34
    developing, 33-34
Merits of position, determining, 18-19
Methods, new and untried, introducing
    into negotiations, 137
Misunderstandings, avoiding by use of
    correspondence, 79
Montgomery, General, 34
Motives of opponent, determining, 94-95

# N

Napoleon, 27
Naturalness, projecting image of, 35-37
    in speaking, 53
Neatness, importance of, 31
    essential in correspondence, 80
Neckties, choice of, 36-37
Negative emotion, anger as, 102
Negotiation, definition of, 18
Never Give In, 129n
New elements, addition of, 136-138
    language, 137
    method for, 137-138
        of methods, new and untried,
            137
    parties, 136
"90 Day Letter," 65-66
Nizer, Louis, 155, 155n
"No," when to take for an answer,
    126-127
    caution, 127
    persistence most important key to
        successful negotiation, 127
Notice of Deficiency, 65-66

# O

Object, using to emphasize point, 38
Objectivity, need for, 56-57

*Objectivity (cont.)*
  essential for negotiator, 105-106
Observation, importance of, 123-125
  facial features, 123-124
  lateral vision, 124-125
Offensive negotiation, 85-88
  what it is, 85-86
  what to do, 88
  when and how to gain, 86-88
    language, concentrating on, 87
Offer, making, 167-169
  guidelines, essential, 167-168
    flexibility, importance of, 168
  initial, who makes, 168-169
  strategies, types of, 169
Opponent, 94-97
  appearance sometimes deceiving, 94
  Golden Rule of negotiation, 97
  motives of, determining, 94-95
  types of, 95-97
    strong, 95-96
    vacillating type, 96
    weak type, 96-97
  underestimation of, avoiding, 94
Opponent's anger, how to deal with,
  105
Organization, pre-negotiation, 58-61
  by folders, 59
  inks, use of different colors of, 59
  over-organizing, avoiding, 61
Others, danger in following advice of,
  174-177
Over-organizing material, avoiding, 61
"Overclosing," avoiding, 191

# P

Parties, new, interjection of, 136
Patience essential for negotiating, 19
Patton, General George S., 85, 86
Persistence most essential key to
  successful negotiating, 127
Personality, principle vs., 128-132
  (see also "Principle vs.
  personality")
Physical appearance of negotiator, 35-38
  clothes, 35-37
    neckties, 36-37
  mannerisms, 37-38
    eye contact, 37-38
    gestures, 37-38

  object, using to emphasize
    point, 38
Physical environment, 30-32
  interruptions, avoiding, 30
  neatness, importance of, 31
Place to negotiate, 23-24
Plato, 195
Pleasant atmosphere essential for
  negotiating success, 157
Positions, clarification or restatement
  of via correspondence, 79
Positive technique only, repetition as,
  135
Positive thinking, importance of, 33-34
Postage, using proper amount of, 80
Practicing Law Institute, 197
Prayer, 198
Pre-negotiation organization, 58-61
  by folders, 59
  inks, use of different colors of, 59
  over-organizing, avoiding, 61
Precedent, setting, 170-173
  what to do after, 172-173
Predictability, 178-182
  avoiding, 181-182
  danger of, greatest, 180
Preparation, thorough, essential for
  negotiator, 19
Pressures of negotiation, how to hold
  up under, 19-20
  bridge of trust, creating, 20
  understanding of self, 20
Price, Dorothy, 129*n*
Primary negotiating base, 68-70
Principle, negotiating, meaning of, 7
Principle vs. personality, 128-132
  both involved, 132
  personality, definition and discovery
    of, 130-131
    what to do, 131-132
  principle, definition and discovery
    of, 128-129
    what to do, 129-130
Priority of senses, 45-48
Procedure, knowledge of, 65-67
Procrastination conducive to non-
  agreement, 190
Prompting action technique for
  closing, 191
Promptness essential in correspondence,
  80-81
*Proverbs,* 74, 74*n*, 198

# Q

Qualities necessary for negotiating, 19
Question method, 141-146
    advantages of, 141
    choice, requiring, 144-145
    conclusion, 146
    descriptive, 142
    general and specific, 141-142
    leading, 142-143
    for obvious answers, 143-144
    successive, 145
        with answers, 145-146
    suggestive, 143

# R

Reading as first step in learning art of
    negotiating, 193
Recognition, appealing to emotions
    through, 151-153
Relevance in humor essential, 187-188
Repetition, experience and, 193-194
    diverse situations, importance of,
        193-194
    reading as first step, 193
    Repetition, influence of in
        negotiation, 133-135
    as positive technique only, 135
Repetitious words, avoiding use of, 75
Resistance, least, following path of,
    147-148
Restatement of positions through
    correspondence, 79
Rommel, General, 34

# S

Secondary bases, 70-72
Self, appealing to, 98-101
    "selves," definition of, 98-99
    "me" and "I," 99
    sincerity absolutely essential,
        98-101
Self-preservation, appealing to emotions
    through, 153-154
"Selves," definition of, 98-99
Seminars, attending to increase
    knowledge, 196-197

Senses, five negotiating, priority of,
    45-48
Silence, 155
Similar words, using too often as
    bad habit, 75
Simplicity, 118-119
    of language essential, 52-53
Sincerity absolute necessity in appeal-
    ing to opponent's "self,"
    98-101
Skill in negotiations, meaning of, 17-20
    merits of position, determining,
        18-19
    qualities necessary, 19
    pressures of negotiating, how to
        hold up under, 19-20
    bridge of trust, creating, 20
    understanding of self, 20
Smile, warmth of, 156-157
Speaking, clear, practicing, 76
Specific questions, 141-142
Stationery, importance of, 80
Stick theory of preparation, 39-44
    in action, 41-42
    basic, 40-41
    outline, 43-44
    refinement, additional, 43-44
Strategy, meaning of, 7
Strong type of opponent, 95-96
Successive questions, 145
    with answers, 145-146
Suggestive questions, 143
Summarizing agreed-upon points, 190
Summarizing technique of closing, 192

# T

Technical area most often encountered
    by negotiator, increasing knowl-
    edge in, 195-196
Technical words, becoming acquainted
    with, 54
Technique, negotiating, meaning of, 7
Techniques, closing, 191-192
    assumption, 191-192
    prompting action, 191
    summarizing, 192
Termination of negotiations,
    intentional, 183-185
    in federal tax area, 183

*Termination of negotiations (cont.)*
 "going to school," opponent's, 184
  ways to detect, 184-185
 "Thinking it over" conducive to non-
  agreement, 190
*Thinking on Your Feet,* 155n
Time to negotiate, 21-22
Timing, importance of, 120-122
Trend of times, increasing knowledge
  of, 196
Troublesome arguments, potentially,
  disposing of, 158-160
 key words, use of, 158-159
"Two tier" conference, 28

# U

Underestimation of opponent, how to
  avoid, 94
Understanding of self as indispensable
  requirement, 20

# V

Vacillating type of opponent, 96

Value, disproportionate, importance
  of, 151
Visibility of demonstrative exhibits,
  ensuring constant, 165-166

# W

Walley, Dean, 129n
Weak type of opponent, 96-97
Wealth, appealing to emotions through,
  150-151
 value as disproportionate, 151
When to negotiate, 21-22
Where to negotiate, 23-24
Who should receive correspondence,
  79-80
Words, key, use of to squelch potentially
  troublesome arguments, 158-159
Words used by negotiator, 52-55
 definiteness of meaning, 54-55
 descriptive, 53-54
 naturalness of, 53
 simple, need for, 52-53
 technical words, becoming
  acquainted with, 54
Written materials, keeping close
  control of, 176